BRIDGING GRADES
8 to 9

Carson Dellosa Education
Greensboro, North Carolina

Caution: Exercise activities may require adult supervision. Before beginning any exercise activity, consult a physician. Written parental permission is suggested for those using this book in group situations. Children should always warm up prior to beginning any exercise activity and should stop immediately if they feel any discomfort during exercise.

Caution: Before beginning any food activity, ask parents' permission and inquire about the child's food allergies and religious or other food restrictions.

Caution: Nature activities may require adult supervision. Before beginning any nature activity, ask parents' permission and inquire about the child's plant and animal allergies. Remind the child not to touch plants or animals during the activity without adult supervision.

Caution: Before completing any balloon activity, ask parents' permission and inquire about possible latex allergies. Also, remember that uninflated or popped balloons may present a choking hazard.

The authors and publisher are not responsible or liable for any injury that may result from performing the exercises or activities in this book.

Summer Bridge®
An imprint of Carson Dellosa Education
PO Box 35665
Greensboro, NC 27425 USA

© 2022 Carson Dellosa Education. Except as permitted under the United States Copyright Act, no part of this publication may be reproduced, stored, or distributed in any form or by any means (mechanically, electronically, recording, etc.) without the prior written consent of Carson Dellosa Education.

Printed in the USA • All rights reserved.

ISBN 978-1-4838-6600-0

04-064241151

Table of Contents

Making the Most of *Summer Bridge Activities*®..iv
Skills Matrix vi
Summer Reading for Everyone viii
Summer Learning Is Everywhere! x

Section I: Monthly Goals and Word List 1
Introduction to Flexibility 2
Activity Pages 3
Science Experiments 43
Social Studies Activities 45
Outdoor Extension Activities 48

Section II: Monthly Goals and Word List 49
Introduction to Strength 50
Activity Pages 51
Science Experiments 91
Social Studies Activities 93
Outdoor Extension Activities 96

Section III: Monthly Goals and Word List 97
Introduction to Endurance 98
Activity Pages 99
Science Experiments 139
Social Studies Activities 141
Outdoor Extension Activities 144

Answer Key..145
Flash Cards
Certificate of Completion

© Carson Dellosa Education

Making the Most of *Summer Bridge Activities*®

This book will help your child review eighth grade skills and preview ninth grade skills. Inside, find lots of resources that encourage your child to practice, learn, and grow while getting a head start on the new school year ahead.

Just 15 Minutes a Day
...is all it takes to stay sharp with learning activities for each weekday, all summer long!

Month-by-Month Organization
Three color-coded sections match the three months of summer vacation. Each month begins with a goal-setting and vocabulary-building activity. You'll also find an introduction to the section's fitness and character-building focus.

Daily Activities
Two pages of activities are provided for each weekday. They'll take about 15 minutes to complete. Activities will help your child practice these skills and more:

- Grammar and usage
- Writing
- Reading comprehension
- Vocabulary
- Algebraic equations
- Determining ratios
- Geometry
- Statistics and probability

© Carson Dellosa Education

Plenty of Bonus Features
...match your child's needs and interests!

Bonus Activities

Social studies activities include explorers, maps, and more—a perfect complement to summer travel. Science experiments invite your child to interact with the world and build critical thinking skills.

Take It Outside!

A collection of fun ideas for outdoor observation, exploration, learning, and play is provided for each summer month.

Special Features

FITNESS FLASH: Quick exercises to develop strength, flexibility, and fitness

CHARACTER CHECK: Ideas for developing kindness, honesty, tolerance, and more

FACTOID: Fun trivia facts

Skill-Building Flash Cards

Cut out the cards at the back of the book. Store in a zip-top bag or punch a hole in each one and thread on a ring. Take the cards along with you for practice on the go.

Certificate of Congratulations

At the end of the summer, complete and present the certificate at the back of the book. Congratulate your child for being well prepared for the next school year.

Skills Matrix

Day	Algebra, Functions, & Ratios	Character Development	Critical Thinking	Data Analysis & Probability	Decimals, Fractions, & Percentages	Fitness	Geometry & Measurement	Grammar	Language Arts	Literary Terms	Multiplication & Division	Parts of Speech	Problem Solving	Reading Comprehension	Science	Social Studies	Vocabulary	Writing
1	★							★							★		★	
2								★	★					★			★	
3	★													★			★	
4	★																★	★
5				★			★	★									★	
6				★				★					★					
7			★					★	★								★	
8				★						★								
9				★				★							★			
10		★		★													★	
11	★								★			★				★		
12									★			★	★					★
13	★							★	★									
14	★											★		★				★
15	★					★				★		★						
16												★	★				★	
17					★			★	★						★			
18	★						★	★							★			
19										★		★		★				
20								★	★					★				★
Bonus			★			★			BONUS PAGES!						★	★		
1	★							★							★		★	
2	★											★		★				
3	★																★	
4				★				★									★	★
5	★							★						★				
6	★								★								★	★
7			★	★	★													
8								★					★	★				
9	★	★												★			★	
10	★											★			★		★	
11	★								★					★				

Skills Matrix

Day	Algebra, Functions, & Ratios	Character Development	Critical Thinking	Data Analysis & Probability	Decimals, Fractions, & Percentages	Fitness	Geometry & Measurement	Grammar	Language Arts	Literary Terms	Multiplication & Division	Parts of Speech	Problem Solving	Reading Comprehension	Science	Social Studies	Vocabulary	Writing
12							★					★		★				
13	★					★		★									★	
14	★							★										
15	★									★		★			★			
16							★							★		★	★	
17								★				★		★				
18	★									★		★		★				
19				★				★		★								★
20	★											★		★				
BONUS PAGES!			★			★	★								★	★		
1	★						★		★								★	
2	★						★										★	★
3										★	★			★				
4	★					★			★								★	
5	★								★			★			★			
6						★	★							★				
7	★													★			★	
8	★																★	★
9							★	★						★	★			
10							★	★		★				★				
11							★							★				★
12							★			★				★				
13	★	★							★						★			
14				★						★								
15	★													★			★	
16				★					★					★	★			
17						★	★		★					★				★
18	★								★					★				
19					★			★	★								★	
20			★				★						★			★		
BONUS PAGES!			★												★	★		

Summer Reading for Everyone

Reading is the single most important skill for school success. Experts recommend that eighth and ninth grade students read for at least 30 minutes each day. Help your child choose several books from this list based on his or her interests. Choose at least one fiction (F) and one nonfiction (NF) title. Then, head to the local library to begin your reading adventure!

If you like comic books and graphic novels...
El Deafo by Cece Bell (F)
I Am Princess X by Cherie Priest (F)

If you like science fiction...
Fahrenheit 451 by Ray Bradbury (F)
The Roar by Emma Clayton (F)

If you like history...
The Book Thief by Markus Zusak (F)
Code Talker by Joseph Bruchac (F)

If you like mysteries...
Girl, Stolen by April Henry (F)
OCDaniel by Wesley King (F)

If you like diverse voices...
Obsessed
  by Allison Britz (NF)
Brown Girl Dreaming
  by Jacqueline Woodson (NF)

If you like animals...
No Better Friend (Young Readers Edition)
  by Robert Weintraub (NF)
Hoot
  by Carl Hiaasen (F)

If you like books about adventure...
The Call of the Wild
  by Jack London (F)
Hatchet
  by Gary Paulsen (F)

If you like biographies...
42 Is Not Just a Number
  by Doreen Rappaport (NF)
The Boy Who Harnessed the Wind
  by William Kamkwamba and Bryan Mealer (NF)

If you like sports...
The Brooklyn Nine
  by Alan Gratz (F)
Maniac Magee
  by Jerry Spinelli (F)

If you like fantasy...
Poisoned
  by Jennifer Donnelly (F)
Percy Jackson and the Olympians series
  by Rick Riordan (F)

If you like science...
Hidden Figures
  by Margot Lee Shetterly (NF)
The Disappearing Spoon
  by Sam Kean (NF)

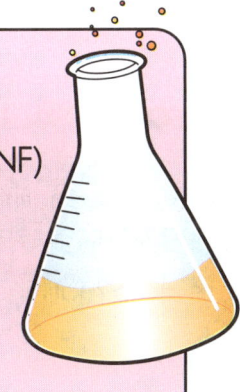

Summer Learning Is Everywhere!

Find learning opportunities wherever you go, all summer long!

Reading

- Read a book that has been adapted for a movie with a friend or family member. Watch the movie together. Compare the book and the movie.
- Read and compare three different versions of the same fairy tale from diverse cultures.

Language Arts

- Create a private blog about your life or your interests.
- Write and mail a letter to a friend or relative telling them about your summer.

Math

- Plan a trip across the country and calculate how much it would cost. Include costs for transportation, hotels, experiences, and food.
- Go on a walk and look for objects with symmetry. Determine how many lines of symmetry each object has. Do you find more manufactured or natural symmetrical objects?

Science & Social Studies

- Create a map of your neighborhood. Include names of streets and any landmarks, such as a school or park.
- Observe the temperature outside every hour during a day. Determine what time of the day is the hottest.

Character & Fitness

- Submit a compliment on a store's website or social media page for an employee that was doing an excellent job.
- Create a morning stretching routine to complete as you wake up each day.

© Carson Dellosa Education

SECTION 1

Monthly Goals

A goal is something that you want to accomplish and must work toward. Sometimes, reaching a goal can be difficult.

Think of three goals to set for yourself this month. For example, you may want to exercise for 30 minutes each day. Write your goals on the lines. Post them somewhere that you will see them every day.

Draw a check mark beside each goal you meet. Feel proud that you have met your goals and continue to set new ones to challenge yourself.

1. _____
2. _____
3. _____

Word List

The following words are used in this section. Use a dictionary to look up each word that you do not know. Then, write three sentences. Use at least one word from the word list in each sentence.

abhor
ceremonial
daunting
fickle
immunity

lapse
restriction
summons
trivial

1. _____
_____
2. _____
_____
3. _____
_____

SECTION I

Introduction to Flexibility

This section includes fitness and character development activities that focus on flexibility. These activities are designed to get you moving and thinking about building your physical fitness and your character. If you have limited mobility, feel free to modify any suggested exercises to fit your individual abilities.

Physical Flexibility

To the average person, *flexibility* means being able to accomplish everyday physical tasks easily, such as bending to tie a shoe. These everyday tasks can be difficult for people whose muscles and joints have not been used and stretched regularly.

Proper stretching allows muscles and joints to move through their full range of motion, which is important for good flexibility. There are many ways that you stretch every day without realizing it. When you reach for a dropped pencil or a box of cereal on the top shelf, you are stretching your muscles. Flexibility is important to your health, so challenge yourself to improve your flexibility consciously. Simple stretches and activities, such as yoga and tai chi, can improve your flexibility. Set a stretching goal for the summer, such as practicing daily until you can touch your toes.

Flexibility of Character

While it is important to have a flexible body, it is also important to be mentally flexible. Being mentally flexible means being open-minded about change. It can be disappointing when things do not go your way, but this is a normal reaction. Think of a time when unexpected circumstances ruined your recent plans. Maybe your mother had to work one weekend, and you could not go to a baseball game with friends because you needed to babysit a younger sibling. How did you deal with the situation?

A large part of being mentally flexible is realizing that there will be situations in life where unforeseen things happen. Often, it is how you react to the circumstances that affects the outcome. Arm yourself with tools to be flexible, such as having realistic expectations, brainstorming solutions to make a disappointing situation better, and looking for good things that may have resulted from the initial disappointment.

Mental flexibility can take many forms. For example, being fair, respecting the differences of other people, and being compassionate are ways that you can practice mental flexibility. In difficult situations, remind yourself to be flexible, and you will reap the benefits of this important character trait.

Functions/Grammar

DAY 1

Write *function* or *not a function* under each table to show whether or not the inputs and outputs represent a function.

1.
Input	Output
0	0
1	1
2	2
3	3

_____

2.
Input	Output
−2	4
−1	2
1	2
2	4

_____

3.
Input	Output
3	5
1	6
1	7
3	8

_____

4.
Input	Output
0	0
0	1
−2	2
3	3

_____

5.
Input	Output
−4	6
−2	10
1	16
2	18

_____

6.
Input	Output
3	5
2	2
1	−1
0	−4

_____

Label each sentence as either a *gerund*, *participle*, or *infinitive* to show the type of verbal used.

7. _____ David thought it was difficult reading the book that he was assigned.

8. _____ Gabe is busy reading one hour each day of the week.

9. _____ Monica's mother called to warn her of the storm.

10. _____ Tomorrow, Molly and Saraya are going hiking.

11. _____ A wrecking ball knocked down the old building.

12. _____ Rashawn loves to surf on big waves with his sister.

13. _____ One of the most popular Olympic sports is swimming.

CHARACTER CHECK: Try to give two people that you see today a compliment.

DAY 1

Vocabulary/Science

Look up each word in an online or print dictionary. Underline the syllable that is stressed. Then, write the word's part of speech and definition on the line. If it has more than one definition and part of speech, then use the first one listed.

14. abhor
    _____
    _____

15. bisect
    _____
    _____

16. conjecture
    _____
    _____

Label the missing lunar phases using the word bank below.

| full moon | waxing gibbous | waning crescent |
| new moon | first quarter | third quarter |

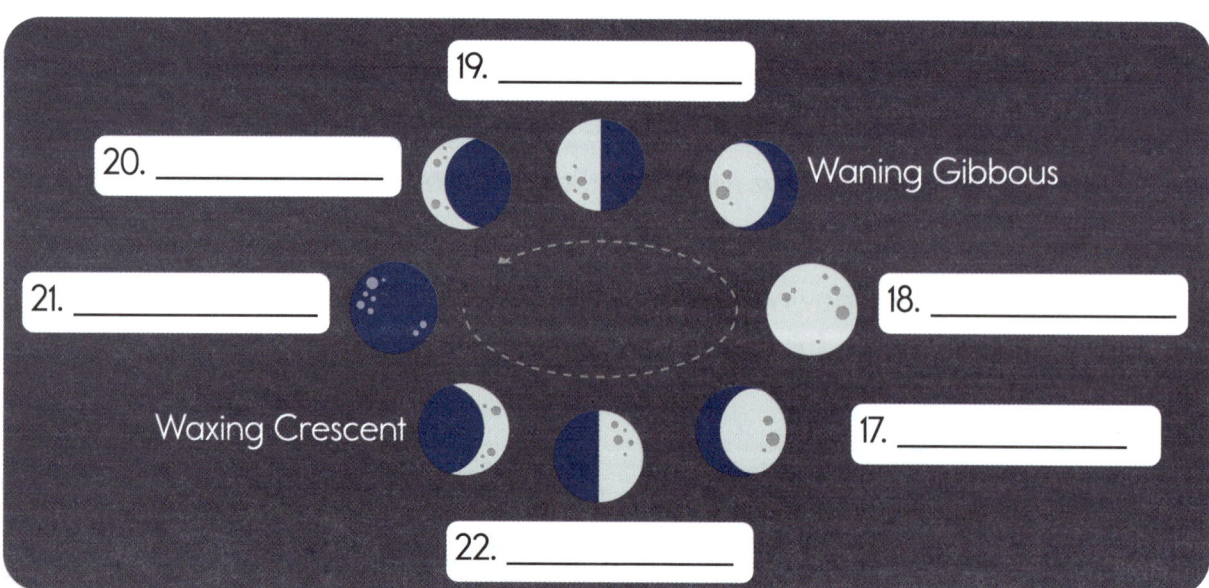

Geometry/Language Arts

DAY 2

Rotate each geometric shape as stated. Draw the rotated figure on the coordinate plane.

1.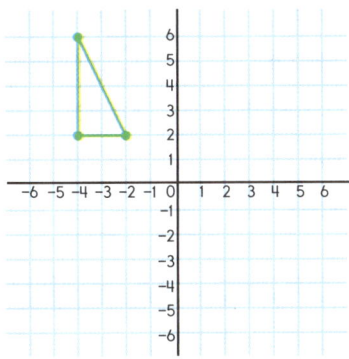
   Rotate 90° clockwise about the origin.

2.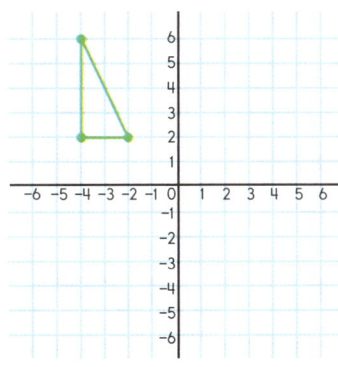
   Rotate 180° clockwise about the origin.

3.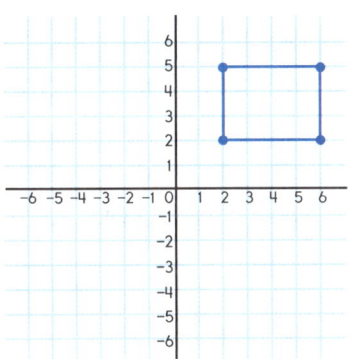
   Rotate 180° clockwise about the origin.

4.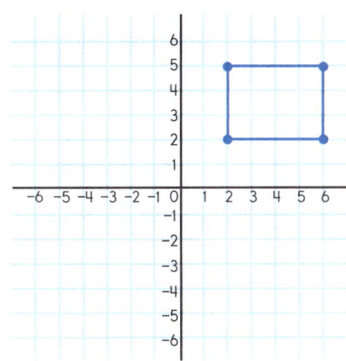
   Rotate 90° clockwise about the origin.

Read each sentence. Add punctuation as needed.

5. The orchardist grows pears cherries and apples.
6. Time seemed to stand still as Laylas mom opened the envelope frowning at the report.
7. The Oz family bought towels shovels and chairs at the shop they carried it all as they ran toward the sandy beach.
8. The pile of laundry never seeming to diminish was constantly taunting Sam.
9. Fall brought cooler temperatures crunching leaves beneath their feet and the aroma of pumpkin spice.

DAY 2

Vocabulary/Reading Comprehension

Choose the word that correctly completes each analogy.

10. dolphin : ocean :: lion :
    A. aquatic   B. carnivore
    C. grassland   D. pride

11. smell : nose :: sound :
    A. ears   B. eyes
    C. hearing   D. sight

12. trivial : relevant :: heroic :
    A. daring   B. slight
    C. timid   D. valiant

13. triangle : three :: octagon :
    A. two   B. four
    C. eight   D. ten

Read the passage. Then, answer the questions.

The Model T

In 1908, Henry Ford introduced the Model T car, which was also known as the "Tin Lizzie." Henry Ford worked to develop a car that was more affordable for people to buy and easier for a company to produce. This was accomplished through mass production and the use of an assembly line during the manufacturing. Mass production helped increase efficiency because employees and machines had a specialty. Prior to the creation of the Model T, owning a car was a **luxury**, and there were fewer than 200,000 cars on the road. From 1908 to 1927, more than 15 million Model T cars were built and sold. The cost of these vehicles started at around $800 and actually decreased as Ford's efficiency on the assembly line increased.

14. What is the main idea of the passage?
    A. Only wealthy people could buy Model T cars.
    B. The Model T changed the automotive industry.
    C. The Model T was better than previous vehicles.

15. Which of the following best defines the word *luxury* as used in this passage?
    A. an extravagance   B. an expense
    C. happiness   D. inexpensive

16. What is the author's purpose in writing this passage?

    _____

    _____

> **FACTOID:** A town in New Zealand has the longest name at 85 letters long. Taumatawhakatangihangakoauauotamateaturipukakapikimaungahoronukupokaiwhenuakitanatahu

Ratios/Vocabulary

DAY 3

Find the unit rate in each problem. Equivalent ratios are provided for the first problem. Solve for the variable.

1. Kiley uses $1\frac{1}{2}$ cups of brown rice flour for 10 servings of gluten-free flour. How much brown rice flour is used in 1 serving? Let x represent the amount of gluten-free flour.

    equivalent ratios: $\frac{x}{1} = \frac{1\frac{1}{2}}{10}$ _____ cup of brown rice flour per serving

2. Chase ran $36\frac{3}{4}$ miles over 6 days. He ran the same distance each day. How many miles did he run each day? Let m represent the number of miles.

    equivalent ratios: _____ miles per day

3. A food truck uses $16\frac{1}{2}$ ounces of french fries for 5 servings. How many ounces of french fries are used in 1 serving? Let f represent the number of ounces of french fries.

    equivalent ratios: _____ ounces of french fries per serving

Choose a word from the word bank to correctly complete each sentence, and write it on the line. Use context clues in the sentence to help.

| ceremonial | fickle | restriction |
| daunting | immunity | summons |

4. Ali shuddered while reading the _____ list of chores to complete.
5. Over time, your body may develop natural _____ to common colds and germs.
6. The manager received a _____ to attend a court hearing.
7. Carlos felt _____ when he could not decide between chocolate or vanilla ice cream.
8. The toddler swing has a recommended weight _____.
9. Ashley bent forward as the _____ crown was placed on her head.

DAY 3

Reading Comprehension

Read the passage. Then, answer the questions.

Charles Darwin

In 1809, Charles Darwin was born in Shrewsbury, England. His father had high hopes that his son would become a doctor. Darwin left his mark on the world in another way by changing the field of science as the world knew it. He became a naturalist, which is a person who studies nature and the environment.

Darwin joined the crew of the British Royal Navy's *HMS Beagle* in 1831 on a voyage to survey the coastline of South America. He studied various plant and animal species on the trip, both in regions of South America and on remote islands, including the Galapagos Islands. He collected specimens and fossils, and he took copious notes and made many drawings that he brought with him back to England to continue his studies.

Through his research, Darwin noticed changes in species over time. He developed his theory of natural selection based most notably on the finches and tortoises he had viewed on the islands. Natural selection dictates that individuals within a species are more likely to survive and reproduce when they inherit genes from parents best suited for an environment. The phrase "survival of the fittest" was coined to describe natural selection.

Darwin believed that species adapt and evolve over time to survive in their surroundings. The strongest in a population are those that are most likely to reproduce, which leads to offspring inheriting the traits that will help them survive.

Darwin's evolutionary theories were **controversial** at the time; but, through scientific evidence that has been collected, the theories have come to be widely accepted and renowned in the scientific community.

10. Which of the following best defines the word *controversial*?
    A. an opinion disbelieved and disliked by some
    B. factually proven
    C. prone to survival
    D. an unquestioned and widely accepted opinion

11. Which is the best explanation of natural selection?
    A. Traits within a population change over time.
    B. Every animal species has developed and adapted from earlier species.
    C. Organisms that are best adapted are more likely to reproduce and pass traits to the next generation.
    D. Some animals in a species are more likely to survive than others.

 **FITNESS FLASH:** Do jumping jacks for 30 seconds.

* See page ii.

Algebra/Vocabulary

DAY 4

Solve each equation. Check your solution by showing that it makes the equation true.

1. $2x = -14$ _____
2. $y - 7 = -3$ _____
3. $4 = a - 6$ _____
4. $\dfrac{x}{6} = -4$ _____
5. $36q = 18$ _____
6. $y + 2 = 45$ _____
7. $18 = \dfrac{s}{4}$ _____
8. $-8 + a = 1$ _____

Choose a word from the word bank to correctly complete each sentence. Use context clues to help. Write the word on the line.

adequate	blemish	haphazard
boon	debris	lapse

9. Because there was not a(n) _____ supply of water in the water jug, the students were all very thirsty.

10. The shirt was on sale because there was a small _____ on the sleeve.

11. Ben and Alex bought smoothies during the _____ of time between the two baseball games.

12. It was hard to find my journal on Mrs. Green's shelf because the books were placed in a(n) _____ way.

13. After the raccoon rummaged through our trash cans, there was _____ scattered all over our lawn.

14. Having dozens of young children in the neighborhood was a huge _____ for the local babysitters.

DAY 4

Vocabulary/Writing

The way a word is used in a sentence can help you determine its meaning. Read each sentence. Circle the correct meaning of each underlined word as it is used in the sentence.

15. When asked to switch topics for the science project, Dylan was <u>flexible</u> and happily agreed.
    A. easily able to change
    B. bending easily without breaking

16. The car company had to stop selling the electric car because there was a <u>defect</u> in the battery.
    A. one who abandons a country or cause
    B. an imperfection or flaw

17. After Mr. Fisher retired, there was a <u>vacancy</u> in the English Department at the high school.
    A. empty space
    B. job opening

18. Ali's favorite <u>accessory</u> is a bright-colored bag.
    A. something added to an outfit to make it more attractive
    B. someone who assists in committing a crime

19. The central <u>artery</u> that goes through downtown Chicago is full of traffic at all hours.
    A. a vessel that carries blood from the heart to the rest of the body
    B. a main road

20. Wes <u>distorted</u> the truth to avoid getting into trouble.
    A. to give a false account of something
    B. to twist out of shape

Imagine what a day would be like from a backpack's point of view. How would the world seem different from your backpack's perspective? Write about it. Use another piece of paper if you need more space.

_____
_____
_____
_____

 **FITNESS FLASH:** Jog in place for 30 seconds.

* See page ii.

Geometry/Probability

DAY 5

Find the length represented by x for each pair of similar triangles.

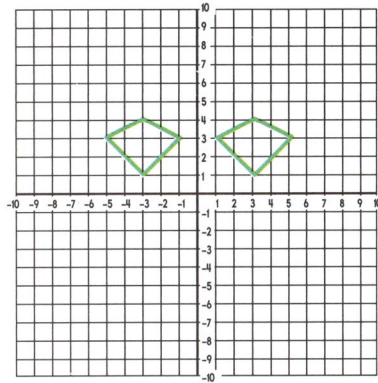

1. Over which line did the reflection take place to create the image?

   _____

2. Point A (5, −1) is reflected over the x-axis. What are the coordinates of the resulting point, A′, after the reflection?

   _____

3. Point B (−2, −4), is reflected over the y-axis. What are the coordinates of the resulting point, B′, after the reflection?

   _____

Find the probability of each event. State your answer as a simplified fraction.

4. A six-sided die has sides that are labeled 1 through 6. What is the probability of rolling a 2 or a 5?

   _____

5. A coin is flipped 2 times. What is the probability of the coin landing on heads 2 times in a row?

   _____

6. A spinner is divided into 8 sections of the same size, and then labeled with the numbers 1 through 8. What is the probability of the spinner landing on an even number?

   _____

DAY 5

Read each word. Write the root word, the prefix, and the suffix in the correct columns. Some words will have either a prefix or a suffix, and some words may have both a prefix and a suffix.

	root word	prefix	suffix
7. lecturer			
8. misjudge			
9. prefabricated			
10. dishonor			
11. immortality			

Downward-Facing Dog

It is likely that at some point in your life, if it has not happened already, you will be asked to participate in a yoga class. Yoga is a great form of stress relief and an excellent way to stay fit. Through a series of physical poses and meditation, yoga helps to improve balance and flexibility. Many of the poses have interesting names. The downward-facing dog is one of the best-known poses and is simple to learn. Its name comes from the fact that the pose resembles a dog stretching with its hind legs.

It is best to perform yoga on a towel or mat. Begin with your hands and knees on the mat, with your palms flat and knees apart. Raise your knees off the mat and lift your tailbone. Pull your hips towards the ceiling. Take deep breaths and exhale as you hold this pose. How do you feel after this pose?

CHARACTER CHECK: What does *empathy* mean? Write about a time when you showed empathy.

Data Analysis/Grammar

DAY 6

Complete the two-way table using the given information.

1. A survey of 126 farmers found that 72 of them planted carrots and 45 planted potatoes. There are 38 farmers that planted both carrots and potatoes, and 47 farmers that did not plant carrots or potatoes.

	Carrots	No Carrots	Total
Potatoes			
No Potatoes			
Total			

2. Of the 350 people at a convention, 80% had a regular pass, while the rest had a premium pass. There were 184 people who stayed for lunch, while the rest did not. Of the people who stayed for lunch, 52 had a premium pass.

	Lunch	No Lunch	Total
Regular Pass			
Premium Pass			
Total			

When the subject of a sentence performs the action, the verb is in the active voice. When the subject of a sentence is being acted upon, the verb is in the passive voice. Rewrite each sentence in the active voice.

3. I was frustrated by last night's math homework.
   _____
   _____

4. The scientists were surprised by the results of the experiment.
   _____
   _____

5. The window was broken by Jack's neighbor Sam.
   _____
   _____

DAY 6

Reading Comprehension

Read the passage. Then, answer the questions.

The Migration of Loggerhead Sea Turtles

Over time, organisms develop adaptations to aid in their survival. A behavioral adaptation of loggerhead sea turtles is their pattern of migration in the open ocean. This occurs shortly after hatching along the shores of the Atlantic Ocean. While the turtle eggs require the security of the sands of the coastline, the hatchlings must vacate quickly to avoid a variety of predators that inhabit the shoreline, such as birds and predatory fish. The loggerhead sea turtles return to their hatching grounds to lay eggs of their own when they are older.

Scientists have long debated how young sea turtles can navigate the waters of the open ocean. Some scientists believed that the turtles spent their complete migration floating in the ocean currents. However, satellite tracking studies in the past few decades have shown evidence to disprove this long-believed idea that the loggerhead sea turtles relied solely on the ocean currents of the Atlantic Ocean to passively transport them to their destination. Scientists now believe that the turtles use the magnetic field of the Earth's core to navigate through their migratory path. It is believed that the turtles are born with the instincts to understand the subtle shifts in the magnetic field, and they use these shifts to guide them. While the loggerhead sea turtles do rely on the currents to allow for passive swimming, they also actively swim when the magnetic field signals them to change course.

Unfortunately, loggerhead sea turtles are listed as endangered species. The more that is understood about their migration patterns, the better the chances that scientists and conservationists will be able to protect these animals from extinction.

6. Why do loggerhead sea turtles migrate from the shores of the Atlantic Ocean?
   A. to find better food sources
   B. too many predators on land
   C. to lay their eggs in the open ocean
   D. the shores are too cold

7. Which is an example of a behavioral adaptation?
   A. talons on an owl
   B. dense fur of an otter
   C. specialized call of a chickadee
   D. sharp teeth of a cheetah

8. How are loggerhead sea turtles able to navigate their migration paths?

   _____

FACTOID: There are pink dolphins that live in the Amazon River.

Geometry/Grammar

DAY 7

Write the coordinates of the pre-image, translate each figure according to the rule given, and write the coordinates of the image. The first translation has been done for you.

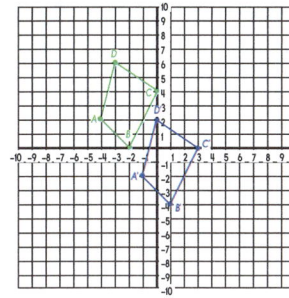

1. Mapping rule: $(x, y) \rightarrow (x + 3, y - 4)$

Pre-image coordinates: A: (–4, 2) B: (–2, 0) C: (0, 4) D: (–3, 6)

Image coordinates:
A': (–1, –2) B': (___ , ___) C': (___ , ___) D': (___ , ___)

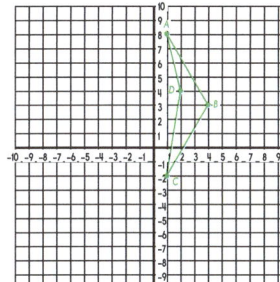

2. Mapping rule: $(x, y) \rightarrow (x - 6, y + 1)$

Pre-image coordinates:
_____

Image coordinates:
_____

A verb in the *indicative mood* expresses a fact or an opinion.
EXAMPLE: I like strawberry ice cream.

A verb in the *imperative mood* expresses a command or a request.
EXAMPLE: Please lock the door behind you when you leave.

A verb in the *interrogative mood* asks a question.
EXAMPLE: Did Antonia join the basketball team?

A verb in the *conditional mood* expresses something that is dependent on a condition.
EXAMPLE: If it rains tomorrow, then we will go to the movie theater.

Read each sentence. Identify the verb mood by writing *I* (indicative), *IM* (imperative), *IN* (interrogative), or *C* (conditional) on the line.

3. _____ Elephants travel in herds.
4. _____ Is Ronan planning to come to Abby's birthday party?
5. _____ Tell your sister that it is time to turn out the light and go to bed.
6. _____ If we have a lemonade stand, then we can donate some money to the animal shelter.
7. _____ Can you take out the trash before it overflows?
8. _____ Watch where you are stepping.
9. _____ Rashida made Brooke a friendship bracelet.
10. _____ Should I offer to mow Ms. Watson's lawn?
11. _____ If the Lions win their next game, then they will be in the playoffs.

DAY 7

Vocabulary/Critical Thinking

Circle the letter next to the word that correctly completes each analogy.

12. adjacent : far :: bankrupt : _____
    A. money   B. wealthy   C. close   D. separate

13. diminish : lessen :: intrude : _____
    A. invade   B. withdraw   C. thief   D. decline

14. sweater : apparel :: _____ : emotion
    A. opinion   B. cry   C. anger   D. reason

15. exquisite : beautiful :: famished : _____
    A. full   B. hungry   C. gorgeous   D. thirsty

16. prefix : word :: _____ : telescope
    A. stargaze   B. suffix   C. astronomer   D. lens

Start with the given word and change one letter as you move up or down each rung of the ladder to create a new word.

liter
17. _____
biker
18. _____
hides
19. _____

CHARACTER CHECK: What is something you can do to show someone that you appreciate them?

Probability/Grammar

DAY 8

Two events are said to be dependent if the outcome of one can affect the outcome or probability of the other. Two events are independent if the outcomes do not affect each other. Answer the questions below.

1. Irina pulls a shirt out of her drawer, checks what color it is, and then pulls another shirt out without putting the first shirt back. Are these events *dependent* or *independent*?

   _____

2. Roger randomly chooses a card from the five cards shown below. Without putting the first card back, he chooses another card.

   What is the probability of Roger choosing a 4 and then a 1? Express your answer as a fraction in lowest terms.

   _____

3. Omar chooses a marble at random from the bag shown below. Without putting the first marble back, he chooses another marble.

   What is the probability that Omar chooses two blue marbles? Express your answer as a fraction in lowest terms.

   _____

Each sentence contains a shift in verb voice or mood. Rewrite the sentence correctly on the line below.

4. Take turns going down the slide and then ate your snack.

   _____

5. As the school bus turned the corner, by the riders a clunking sound was heard.

   _____

6. She goes to the grocery store and bought some snacks.

   _____

7. Take a picture and then you should make the memory last.

   _____

DAY 8

Literary Terms

An *idiom* is a phrase that has a different meaning than the literal meaning of each word within the expression. Underline the idiom in each sentence. Then, write what you think the idiom means.

8. After scoring a 95% on his math test, Evan was excited to tell his parents that he passed with flying colors.
   _____

9. It is supposed to rain for the party tomorrow and, to add fuel to the fire, the rental company is all out of tents!
   _____

10. Sophia is still up in the air as to whether she will come to the softball game on Wednesday.
    _____

11. When Raphael went back to finish college at age 60, he felt like a fish out of water.
    _____

12. Monica was very hungry, so she helped herself to a lion's share of the pizza.
    _____

13. We are down to the wire with our fundraising project; we only have 24 hours left to raise all the money we need for the new playground.
    _____

14. Josh said he was sad that today was his last day of work at the paint shop, but we all knew he was crying crocodile tears.
    _____

15. Jesse and Nicole are on the same page about cell phone rules for their children; both said that phones are not allowed at the dinner table.
    _____

FITNESS FLASH: Do arm circles for 30 seconds.

* See page ii.

Probability/Grammar

DAY 9

Determine the probability of each event.

1. A tray has 16 doughnuts, 9 of which contain raspberry jam and 7 of which contain lemon curd. What is the probability that Ling randomly selects a doughnut with raspberry jam and then Alexander randomly selects a doughnut with lemon curd?
   _____

2. Marnie makes necklaces from beads of the same size and shape. She has a container of 30 beads, with an equal number of blue, red, and yellow beads. What is the probability that she randomly selects a blue bead, puts it back in the container, and then randomly selects a blue bead again?
   _____

3. LaMarcus flips a quarter and then flips a dime. What is the probability that both of the coins will land on heads?
   _____

4. An art class has 18 students, including Naoko and Samir. The students write their names on slips of paper and place them into a hat. Two slips will be selected from the hat without replacement. What is the probability that both Naoko and Samir will be selected?
   _____

Read the passage. Draw a line under each word that should be capitalized.

5. In 1775, the continental congress appointed the first postmaster general. The person was a historical figure who was familiar to most people: benjamin franklin. Franklin helped to organize and develop the united states postal service, which is still in operation today, more than 200 years later. The first postage stamps were issued in 1847. In 1860, as the united states was expanding west, the pony express was born. Over time, the U.S. postal service has continued to adapt, and letter carriers still work to deliver mail around the world today.

DAY 9

Reading Comprehension

Read the passage. Then, answer the questions.

The Lost City of Pompeii

In 79 A.D., the Roman Empire experienced one of the most famous volcanic eruptions in history. In Italy, just south of today's Naples, Mount Vesuvius, a long-dormant volcano, erupted. Smoke, ash, and poisonous fumes soared 20 miles into the air before devastating the lands around Vesuvius, including the wealthy Roman town of Pompeii. Very quickly, Pompeii and Herculaneum, another town close to Vesuvius, were completely covered by a thick layer of volcanic ash. Estimates show that about 16,000 people died in the region, with 2,000 having perished in Pompeii alone.

Pompeii was forgotten for centuries. Then, in 1748, explorers started digging near Vesuvius and made an incredible discovery. To their amazement, they found that the volcanic ash had created a time capsule. Since the disaster had happened so quickly, life was captured under the ash and preserved. Buildings were kept intact that otherwise would have fallen into ruin over the course of centuries. Skeletons of Vesuvius's victims were found buried in the ash as if they were frozen in time. Everyday goods were found scattered about the streets. Archaeologists have even found jars containing preserved food such as fruit and bread. Pompeii has taught modern people much about what life was like for ordinary people of the Roman Empire.

Even though excavations began on Pompeii in 1748, about a third of the city still remains buried. However, archaeologists are more concerned with preserving what has been discovered than with digging up more. Pollution, tourism, and the regular impact of the weather put Pompeii at risk. As a result, archaeologists have slowed new findings to cautiously ensure that this remarkable historical site may continue to be preserved for centuries to come.

6. Which of these events occurred last?
   A. eruption of Vesuvius
   B. tourists impacting Pompeii
   C. burial of Pompeii under ash
   D. discovery of ruins near Vesuvius

7. What are archaeologists at Pompeii most concerned about today?
   A. making new discoveries
   B. finding the cause of the disaster
   C. preserving old findings
   D. locating where to excavate

8. How have the archaeological discoveries at Pompeii contributed to our understanding of the past?

   _____
   _____
   _____

Probability/Grammar

DAY 10

Imagine rolling a 6-sided number cube. Fill out each Venn diagram with the appropriate outcomes, then explain why the two events are disjoint or overlapping. Part of number 1 has been completed for you.

1. Event A: rolling a 1
   Event B: rolling an even number

   Event A: 1
   Event B: 2, 6, 4
   Outside: 3, 5

   Are these events disjoint or overlapping? Why? _____

2. Event A: rolling a number greater than 5
   Event B: rolling an odd number

   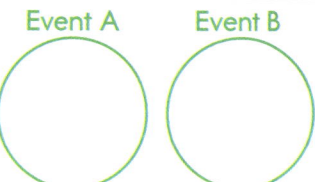

   Are these events disjoint or overlapping? Why? _____

3. Event A: rolling a 1, 2, or 4
   Event B: rolling a prime number

   Are these events disjoint or overlapping? Why? _____

Read each sentence. Add commas where they are needed.

4. After the winter storm it was difficult to walk up the slippery steep driveway.
5. While I was finishing my breakfast the school bus arrived.
6. I was born in Rochester New York on January 28 2006.
7. Before she leaves for baseball Leila packs her bag with a water bottle her baseball glove her helmet and her bat.
8. Ani was exhausted from a long day of school and babysitting but he had to finish his homework before he could go to sleep.
9. Dylan please take your shoes off before coming inside.
10. *Divergent* a book by Veronica Roth takes place in the future.

DAY 10

Vocabulary/Character Development

Choose the vocabulary word from the word bank that best completes each sentence, and write it on the line.

| evoke | bisect | novice |
| authority | integrate | simulate |

11. The geometry teacher decided to _____ some art into his math lesson by asking students to design a robot out of various shapes.
12. The _____ track meet was for athletes who had never run competitively before.
13. At the science museum, there are two machines that _____ the feeling of hurricane-force winds.
14. Teresa made sure to _____ the cookie so that her sister and her brother would each get an equal share.
15. The goal of the documentary was to _____ feelings of shock and surprise in the audience.
16. The principal used her _____ to make the final decision about the new school mascot.

Being Generous

Generosity refers to the quality of being kind and generous. A person who is generous gives to others and acts selflessly. Read the situations below. Choose one. Draw a three-panel comic strip showing characters before, during, and after the situation. Be sure to include a caption for each panel.

- A student sees a sign that a local shelter is collecting board games for their visitors to play. The student realizes that he has many board games. The student chooses some favorites to give away that he thinks the shelter's visitors might enjoy. The student is displaying generosity by being selfless and giving to others.

- A teenager and her little brother buy ice cream at a shop. The little brother drops his ice cream before he even gets to taste it. The teenager helps him clean up the mess and shares her ice cream with her little brother. The teenager is displaying generosity by sharing with her little brother.

FACTOID: Hawaii became the 50th state of the United States on August 21, 1959.

Functions/Parts of Speech

DAY 11

Compare each pair of functions. Complete each statement using the words *greater than*, *less than*, or *equal to*.

1. Function A

x	1	2	3	4
y	4	7	10	13

   Function B: $y = -2x + 3$

   The slope of Function A is _____ the slope of Function B.

2. Function A

x	–3	3	6	15
y	–1	–3	–4	–7

   Function B:

   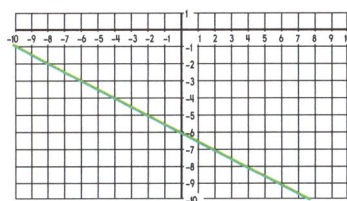

   The slope of Function A is _____ the slope of Function B.

A *personal pronoun* takes the place of a person, place, or thing. An *indefinite pronoun* refers generally to a person or a thing. A *demonstrative pronoun* refers to a specific person or thing. Underline the pronoun in each sentence and identify it. Write *P* for personal, *I* for indefinite, or *D* for demonstrative.

3. _____ Dion arrived at the game before you did.
4. _____ Is there anyone who knows how to sew a button on this coat?
5. _____ Alex knew about that before Mattie did.
6. _____ Nobody volunteered to run for class president.
7. _____ Those are the books Coleman should read during winter break.
8. _____ Can we review the study sheet before the test?
9. _____ Almost everyone who tried the corn maze could not find the way out.
10. _____ This is the quickest way to Nicole's house.
11. _____ Ask Jacob to meet us at the entrance to the museum.
12. _____ Most of the people at the picnic were eating sandwiches.

DAY 11

Language Arts/Social Studies

Select the word that is spelled correctly.

13. A. strawberries   B. strawberryes   C. strawberrys
14. A. defishent   B. deficient   C. deficeint
15. A. beautifull   B. beautyful   C. beautiful
16. A. aerial   B. airial   C. aereal
17. A. personification B. personificashun C. personifikation
18. A. defendent   B. defendant   C. defendint

Understanding Hemispheres on Maps

If you look at a globe, then you will understand that the world is divided into four *hemispheres*. Each hemisphere contains half the world, either north and south or east and west. Hemispheres are used to help people understand the location of geographical points on Earth in relation to other points, especially continents. Hemispheres are divided by imaginary lines of latitude and longitude. The line that divides the Northern Hemisphere and the Southern Hemisphere, for example, is called the *equator*. The Eastern Hemisphere and the Western Hemisphere are divided by two lines of longitude: the prime meridian at 0 degrees longitude and the international date line at 180 degrees longitude.

Use an atlas or globe to answer the following questions.

19. Which continent lies in both the Northern Hemisphere and the Southern Hemisphere?
    A. Antarctica
    B. Australia
    C. Asia
    D. Africa

20. Which continent is located in the Western Hemisphere?
    A. North America
    B. Europe
    C. Africa
    D. Antarctic

21. Which two continents are located entirely in the Southern Hemisphere?

_____

CHARACTER CHECK: Give yourself a compliment today.

Problem Solving/Parts of Speech

DAY 12

Solve each problem.

1. On Monday, 5,800 people visited a website. On Tuesday, 10% more people visited the website than on Monday. How many people visited the website on Tuesday?
   _____ people

2. The cost of a hotel room during the peak season is $150. The cost is 35% less during the off-peak season. What is the cost of the hotel room during the off-peak season?
   $ _____

3. A project is originally scheduled to take 25 days. The project manager decides to increase the number of days by 20%. How many days is the project scheduled to take now?
   _____ days

When the subject of a sentence performs the action, the verb is in the active voice. When the subject of a sentence is being acted upon, the verb is in the passive voice. Read each sentence. If the verb is in the active voice, then write *AV*. If the verb is in the passive voice, then rewrite the sentence in the active voice.

4. For my last birthday, I was given a bicycle by my parents. _____
   _____

5. I try to read the Declaration of Independence every Fourth of July. _____
   _____

6. The dog seemed sorry that it dug up the garden. _____
   _____

7. The audience was amazed by the magician's tricks. _____
   _____

8. Every Thanksgiving, Juan's pecan pie is gobbled up by the guests. _____
   _____

FACTOID: Australia has more sheep than it does people.

DAY 12

Literary Terms/Writing

Choose a word from the word bank to correctly complete each sentence, and write the word on the line.

| poetry | drama | autobiography |
| historical fiction | fable | myth |

9. A(n) _____ is written with stage directions and dialogue, and is performed as a play.
10. _____ is written in verse with vivid imagery that creates emotional responses.
11. In a(n) _____, the characters are usually talking animals, and the purpose of the story is to teach a lesson or truth.
12. A(n) _____ is a true story about a person's life, and it is written by that person.
13. A(n) _____ is a traditional story within a culture used to explain some kind of mystery or phenomenon. The characters are often gods or goddesses.
14. _____ is a story that is set in the past, with accurate details of a specific time and place.

Describe your favorite sandwich. Explain the step-by-step instructions that someone could use to make your sandwich. Be sure to be very detailed and descriptive in your instructions. Use another piece of paper if you need more space.

_____
_____
_____
_____
_____
_____
_____

FITNESS FLASH: Bend over and touch your toes. Hold it for 5 seconds. Then stand upright again. Do this 15 times.

* See page ii.

Algebra/Geometry

DAY 13

Find the value of the variable in each equation.

1. $5h + 7 = -h + 55$ _____
2. $9w + 10w - 7 - w = 83$ _____
3. $-4c + c = 6c + 28 - 2c$ _____
4. $16r + 8 = 24 - 2r$ _____
5. $7 = 93 + 10t - 8t$ _____
6. $54 - q + 11q = 5q - 3q + 14$ _____
7. $-z = 6z - 29 - 5z - 1$ _____
8. $102 = 19 + 8s - 3s + 3$ _____

Two figures are congruent if one can be obtained from the other using a sequence of rotations, reflections, or translations. Show that each pair of figures is congruent by describing one or more transformations that can be used to obtain the second figure from the first.

9.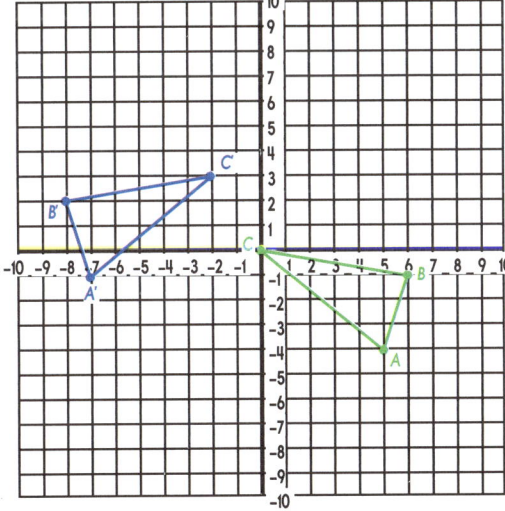

Sequence of transformations:

_____

_____

_____

10.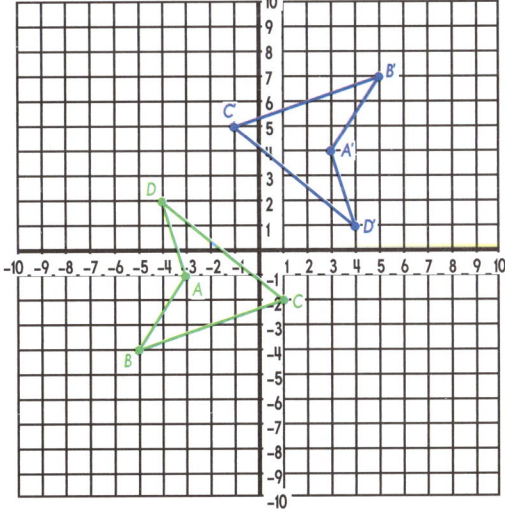

Sequence of transformations:

_____

_____

_____

DAY 13

Language Arts

Read the playbill. Then, answer the questions.

A Tale of Two Moons
by Kristopher Stevens

Cast: (in order of appearance)
Steven Armstrong
Sara Armstrong
Mr. Armstrong
Mrs. Armstrong
News reporter 1
News reporter 2
NASA scientist 1
NASA scientist 2

ACT I

Time: late evening
Setting: July 2025, in the Armstrongs' backyard

Steven and Sara Armstrong are stargazing in their backyard. Sara suddenly notices what appears to be another moon in the distance, and she shows her brother. They excitedly get their parents from the house to show them.

ACT II

Time: early evening
Setting: July 2025, in the Armstrongs' backyard

The Armstrongs are in their backyard with news reporters and NASA scientists, anxiously awaiting darkness. Each of them wants to be a **witness** to the discovery of a second moon.

11. How many characters are in the play?
    A. 4
    B. 6
    C. 8
    D. 10

12. What does the word *witness* mean as it is used in the playbill?
    A. a person in a court case
    B. a person who sees an event
    C. a person who causes an event
    D. a person who acts in a play

13. What is the setting for Act II? _____

FACTOID: Jupiter has 79 moons. Earth has 1 moon.

Algebra/Parts of Speech

DAY 14

Simplify each expression.

1. $3a(2b) + 4ab - 2a =$ _____
2. $6x + 6(2x+y) - 2x - y =$ _____
3. $3n^2 - 2n^2 + n + n(3n) =$ _____
4. $a^2 - 2a^2b + 2a^2 + 2a^2b + 3a^2 =$ _____
5. $8c(2c) + 3b(b) + (-7c^2) =$ _____
6. $x(5x) + 4x + (-3y) - 2(3x^2) - 2y =$ _____

A pronoun in the nominative case is a subject, a predicate nominative, or an appositive. A pronoun in the objective case is the object of a verb or a preposition. Circle the pronoun in parentheses that correctly completes each sentence. Then, identify its case by writing N for nominative and O for objective.

7. _____ Can you tell (we, us) the story again?

8. _____ Katie and (she, her) are going to the park on Saturday.

9. _____ My sister and (I, me) are starting a book drive.

10. _____ I am going to nominate (they, them) to be co-presidents of the chess club.

11. _____ They know that (he, him) is the fastest runner on the team.

12. _____ Matteo and (he, him) will meet you on the soccer field.

13. _____ The museum asked (we, us) to check our coats and backpacks.

14. _____ The school gave Joey and (I, me) an award for community service.

15. _____ When it is spring again, (they, them) will go strawberry picking.

16. _____ Please give the key to the supply closet to (she, her).

 **FITNESS FLASH:** Lie on your back with your feet in the air and pretend to pedal a bike for 1 minute.

* See page ii.

DAY 14

Reading Comprehension/Writing

Read the passage. Then, answer the questions.

The Iditarod

In January 1925, Nome, Alaska, was struck hard by an outbreak of diphtheria. As the respiratory disease spread, the only doctor of the town, Curtis Welch, called for a batch of lifesaving serum from Anchorage. Wilderness and winter conditions made the task seemingly impossible. Alaska's governor, Scott C. Bone, organized teams of dogsled drivers who dared to make the 1,000-mile journey, facing blizzards and temperatures below 60 degrees F, to save the people of Nome.

More than 20 drivers using more than 150 dogs took part in the adventure, which ended when frostbitten driver Gunnar Kassen arrived with the serum in Nome on February 2 with his team led by the dog Balto.

In honor of this feat, Alaska started hosting an annual dogsled race to commemorate the event. The first race took place in 1967. This epic event—a 1,100-mile race between Nome and Anchorage—is called the Iditarod, named after the old dogsled mail route that the race path partially follows.

17. What was the original cause that led to the 1,000-mile journey for the dogsled drivers?
    A. freezing temperatures
    B. spreading disease
    C. ferocious blizzards
    D. daring dogsled drivers

18. Why would Balto be more famous than other dogs who took part in the 1925 dogsled trip?_____

Imagine you are walking along the beach one day, and you find a message in a bottle. What do you think the message would say, and what would your response be? Use another piece of paper if you need more space.

_____
_____
_____
_____
_____

Algebra/Parts of Speech

DAY 15

Use the distributive property to solve the following equations.

1. $3(2x + 5) = 57$ _____
2. $-2(-4x + 3) = 18$ _____
3. $5(-3x - 7) = -5$ _____
4. $2(2x + 6) = 4(x + 3)$ _____
5. $-(5x + 6) = -1$ _____
6. $3(2x + 5) = 2(x + 5) + 4x + 5$ _____

A *relative pronoun* connects a group of words to a noun or pronoun. An *interrogative pronoun* introduces a question. Read each sentence. Write *R* if the underlined pronoun is relative. Write *I* if the underlined pronoun is interrogative.

7. _____ <u>Who</u> will share this pumpkin muffin with me?

8. _____ Grace was not sure <u>what</u> to do with the extra balloons after the party.

9. _____ My English teacher, <u>who</u> has been at the school for 40 years, will be retiring soon.

10. _____ The actor <u>who</u> played the main character in that movie is my second cousin.

11. _____ In <u>whichever</u> art class you choose, make sure that you will be able to paint.

12. _____ <u>What</u> did the class have to read over the summer?

13. _____ I can bring <u>whatever</u> you like for dessert.

14. _____ Please ask <u>whomever</u> is coming to the party not to bring a gift.

15. _____ <u>Which</u> season is your favorite?

16. _____ The *Spirit of St. Louis*, <u>which</u> flew across the Atlantic Ocean in 1927, is now on display in a museum.

DAY 15

Literary Terms/Fitness

Nonfiction writing should be factual and free of bias and personal opinion. Elements of bias may include loaded words, generalizations, and stereotypes. Read the following essay and underline the elements of bias.

The Two Coasts

The United States has two coasts on opposite sides of the country—one along the Atlantic Ocean and one along the Pacific Ocean. These coasts are aptly named the East Coast and the West Coast. The West Coast is made up of California, Oregon, and Washington, while the East Coast is made up of 14 states that border the Atlantic. The West Coast experiences a relatively mild climate year round. Most of the states along the East Coast experience all four seasons.

Other than differences in physical location, there are differences in how people in these regions behave. People on the East Coast are thought of as more uptight and fast paced, while people on the West Coast are more liberal and casual. There are differences in types of food eaten on both coasts too. West Coast diners favor organic and healthier options, whereas East Coast diners favor fast food and carb-laden options.

Because both coasts are near an ocean, they are filled with people who enjoy the coastal regions for recreation and plentiful seafood. Regardless of your coastal preference, we can agree that anyone who lives near the beach is lucky.

Juggling

Juggling is not something you would expect to see in a fitness activity, but you may be surprised by how many benefits there are to learning to juggle. Juggling strengthens both your brain and your body. It helps improve coordination and relieves stress, all while getting you moving. Juggling is also a great party trick.

When learning to juggle, start by using something soft. Beanbags or rolled-up pairs of socks are great options. You can follow these steps to get started:

- Begin by tossing one ball from hand to hand, keeping your eyes on the ball and tossing it slowly and steadily.
- Add a second ball, holding each ball in a different hand. Toss the first ball up. When it reaches its peak, toss the second one into the air.
- Continue practicing this until you feel comfortable.
- Try adding a third ball when you are ready. Hold two balls in your dominant hand and one in your other hand. Throw the one ball from your non-dominant hand into the air, and then throw one of the balls in your dominant hand into the air. Catch the balls and continue throwing.
- Think of throwing the balls in a sideways figure-eight motion.

This takes practice, so keep trying and don't give up!

Problem Solving/Vocabulary

DAY 16

Solve each problem.

1. Hanna bought 5 batteries for $24.98 each. Shipping for all of the batteries costs $11.10. What is the total cost?

   _____

2. A stack of paper includes 100 sheets that are each 0.13 millimeters thick and 100 sheets that are each 0.18 millimeters thick. How thick, in millimeters, is the entire stack of paper?

   _____

3. Jamail collects 3 bags of sand that weigh 13 pounds, 14 pounds, and 17 pounds. He puts an equal amount of the sand into 4 small aquariums. How many pounds of sand did Jamail put into each aquarium?

   _____

Use a print or online thesaurus to find a synonym for each word below. Write the synonym on the line.

4. unattractive
   _____

5. bold
   _____

6. generous
   _____

7. frail
   _____

8. assertive
   _____

9. contempt
   _____

10. identical
    _____

11. pamper
    _____

12. shun
    _____

13. virtue
    _____

DAY 16

Reading Comprehension

Read the passage. Then, answer the questions.

The Human Genome Project

On October 1, 1990, a monumental undertaking began. The Human Genome Project (HGP) was officially underway. An international team of scientists, led by the U.S. National Academy of Sciences, set out with a goal of sequencing and mapping the human genome, the complete set of deoxyribonucleic acid (DNA) for *Homo sapiens*. The HGP took just over 12 years to complete, and the final sequence was published in April 2003.

The scientists involved in the HGP hailed from many countries, including China, France, Germany, Japan, the United Kingdom, and the United States. Samples of DNA were collected through blood samples from many different volunteers and were kept anonymous throughout the entire process. The information learned through this project is public knowledge and is not considered an invention or individual discovery. More information is continuously added to the data set and shared with the world as it becomes available.

The goal of the HGP was to better understand the 20,500 genes that make up the human genome. Scientists were able to determine the order of base pairs along the genome, map the location of gene sections on specific chromosomes, and create linkage maps to track traits through generations. With this knowledge, scientists continue to gain understanding of ways to identify and treat genetic diseases. Because scientists can trace genetic markers through generations, they can better understand why certain traits are expressed and others are suppressed, and they can determine the likelihood that a child will inherit certain traits.

14. How many countries were involved in the Human Genome Project?
    A. two
    B. four
    C. six
    D. nine

15. What is the scientific name for the human species?
    A. *Canis lupus*
    B. *Homo sapiens*
    C. *Felis catus*
    D. *Gorilla beringei*

16. Why are the results of the Human Genome Project important? _____
_____
_____

Decimals & Fractions/Grammar

DAY 17

Rewrite each decimal number as a fraction or mixed number.

1. 9.73 _____
2. 0.862 _____
3. 0.$\overline{47}$ _____
4. 7.15 _____
5. 5.2 _____
6. 0.9$\overline{2}$ _____
7. 3.$\overline{4}$ _____
8. 13.1 _____

An ellipsis is a set of three dots (...) used in a text. An ellipsis can be used to show the passage of time, imply an unfinished thought, or indicate where text was removed from a quotation. Read each sentence. Write *P* if the ellipsis is used to show the passage of time. Write *U* if the ellipsis is used to imply an unfinished thought. Write *Q* if the ellipsis is used to indicate where text was removed from a quotation.

9. _____ A well-known scientist once said, "Life is like riding a bicycle … keep moving."

10. _____ "I might," my friend said, "be able to help you with your homework. … Actually, I'm sorry, I won't have time."

11. _____ When the reporter asked the candidate about her position on the issue, the candidate replied, "I'm not sure …"

12. _____ Mrs. Maple waited for the children to get in line after recess … and eventually led them all back into the classroom.

13. _____ The words of the Gettysburg Address—"Four score and seven years ago our fathers brought forth, upon this continent, a new nation …" —were written by Abraham Lincoln.

FITNESS FLASH: Do 5 lunge squats to the right and 5 to the left.

* See page ii.

DAY 17

Literary Terms/Social Studies

Choose a term from the word bank that matches each description, and write the term on the line.

characterization	setting	simile	foreshadowing	inference
protagonist	plot	personification	symbol	conflict

14. _____ the sequence of events in a story
15. _____ a person or object that represents something else
16. _____ a comparison between two unlike things using *like* or *as*
17. _____ the main character in a literary text
18. _____ giving human qualities to an object or animal
19. _____ hints that something will happen in a story
20. _____ a conclusion drawn from the facts in a text
21. _____ the way an author describes the characters in a story
22. _____ a struggle faced by a character in a literary text
23. _____ the time and place in which a story takes place

Choose a term from the word bank that matches each description, and write the term on the line.

scarcity	supply	demand	recession	resources
monopoly	capitalism	consumer	labor	capital

24. _____ the work needed to make a product
25. _____ the limit of materials available used by people
26. _____ materials used by people either directly or to make products
27. _____ how much people desire certain goods or products
28. _____ control of an entire industry by a single organization
29. _____ the amount of goods or other materials that is available to use
30. _____ a person who uses goods or services
31. _____ an economic downturn
32. _____ an economic system with little government control
33. _____ money or resources used toward creating products

Algebra/Grammar

DAY 18

Solve each inequality. Be sure to check your answer.

1. $4x - 7 > 5$ _____
2. $-2x + 3 < 7$ _____
3. $5x - 2 \geq -17$ _____
4. $3x + 5 < -7$ _____
5. $\frac{x}{4} - 2 \geq 10$ _____
6. $-3x + 7 \geq 1$ _____

Read the paragraph. There are seven words that are spelled incorrectly in the paragraph. Circle each word that is spelled incorrectly, and write the correct spelling above it.

The famous restaurant critic, the Mystery Diner, wrote this review of Chef Roland's new restaurant, Happy Pan: "I have eaten anonamously at Happy Pan restaurant on three seperate occasions, and I was never disatisfied with my meals there. First of all, the service I recieved was extraordinary; even when I was late for my reservation, the staff did their best to accomodate me. And the food, of course, was outragously delicious. I recommend this restaurant enthusiastically and predict a long and successfull career for Chef Roland."

FACTOID: The oldest animal in the world is a Seychelles giant tortoise who lives on the island of Saint Helena and is reported to be about 189 years old!

DAY 18

Geometry/Science

Each set of figures is congruent. How many degrees of clockwise rotation would move the first figure to the second figure?

7.

8.

9.

_____   _____   _____

Read the following passage on the electromagnetic spectrum, and review the word bank. Write the letter of the word from the word bank that completes each sentence. Not all words will be used.

A. gamma rays	D. visible light	G. radiation	J. shortest
B. X-rays	E. infrared	H. sun	K. highest
C. ultraviolet rays	F. radio waves	I. longest	L. lowest

The electromagnetic spectrum shows the range of energy found in _____. This energy naturally comes from the _____, but humans have also created ways to produce different types. For example, light bulbs produce _____. Car stereos use _____. Broken bones are examined using _____.

Gamma rays have the _____ wavelength, which means they have the _____ amount of energy. On the other end of the spectrum, radio waves have the _____ wavelength, which means they have the _____ amount of energy.

FACTOID: Blue jeans were first invented in 1873 by Levi Strauss.

Multiplication & Division/Parts of Speech

DAY 19

Rewrite each multiplication or division expression using a base and an exponent.

1. $3^3 \times 3^2 =$ _____
2. $6^5 \div 6^2 =$ _____
3. $2^{-4} \div 2^2 =$ _____
4. $7^3 \times 7^3 =$ _____
5. $8^8 \div 8^2 =$ _____
6. $(2^{-4})^4 =$ _____
7. $5^3 \div 5 =$ _____
8. $(3^5)^4 =$ _____

Read the paragraph. Circle the pronouns that correctly complete the sentences. Then, reread the paragraph.

Madison and (her, she) brother Karl were getting a dog. Madison wanted a golden retriever, but Karl did not agree; (him, his) heart was set on a poodle. (Them, They) argued about the dog for weeks, but neither one of (them, they) would budge. Finally, (their, theirs) mother had an idea and called up all the rescue shelters in the area until (her, she) found what (her, she) was looking for. Madison and Karl were both thrilled when (their, they) mother brought home a dog that was a bit of what (them, they) both wanted: a goldendoodle.

CHARACTER CHECK: What are two things you like about your best friend?

DAY 19

Read the passage. Then, answer the questions.

Skateboarding

Some people think of skateboarding as a **nuisance** activity, but the 2020 Summer Olympics (held in 2021 in Tokyo) hoped to change that viewpoint. This was the first year that skateboarding was an Olympic event, with females and males as young as 12 years old competing.

The origin of skateboarding is not completely clear, but it seems to have its early roots in the 1950s in California and Hawaii. Surfers wanted to mimic the feel of riding waves when not in the ocean. Wheels were added to short surfboards in those early years. Over time, the boards were adapted. By 1962, the first skateboards were being industrially produced. Skateboarding gained popularity across the United States. With the newfound popularity came new approaches. Skateboarding no longer was just a form of cruising or transportation; some skateboarders began using their boards to do tricks.

The design of skateboards continued to evolve, and they became lighter and more suitable for tricks. By the 1970s, skateboarding was attracting interest around the world. In 1978, the *ollie* was achieved by skateboarder Alan Gelfand. An ollie is when the boarder kicks the tail of the board down, and the board pops into the air with its rider.

Thanks to other greats, like Tony Hawk, skateboarding has been revolutionized and is a sport that many children try at least once. Skate parks where tricks can be practiced have been built in many cities. As even more exposure is gained through events such as the Olympics, skateboarding is a sport that is not going away anytime soon.

9. Which word best defines the term *nuisance* as it is used in the passage?
   A. competitive   B. irritant   C. popular   D. radical

10. Why was skateboarding likely developed?
    A. People were looking for a new sport to compete in.
    B. People wanted to find a similar feeling to surfing but on land.
    C. A new form of transportation was needed.
    D. A new Olympic event needed to be created.

11. Have you ever skateboarded? If so, what do you like or dislike about it?

_____

_____

Problem Solving/Language Arts

DAY 20

Solve each problem.

1. Mr. Olsen lives in Town A. He needs to drive to Town B and then to Town C. The distance between Town A and Town B is 39.23 kilometers, and the distance from Town B to Town C is 94.1 kilometers. There is a direct route from Town A to Town C that is 112.93 kilometers. How many more kilometers does Mr. Olsen need to drive compared to the direct route?

   _____ kilometers

2. Juwan buys 500 toys for $7.45 each and sells them all for $11.99 each. How much profit does Juwan make from selling the toys?

   $_____

3. Sofia and 5 friends buy 3 pizzas. Each pizza costs $13. Sofia and her friends each pay the same amount. How much does each person pay?

   $_____

Possessive adjectives show ownership and do not include an apostrophe. These are sometimes confused with *contractions*, which are shortened forms of a pronoun and verb and do contain an apostrophe. Circle the word in parentheses that correctly completes each sentence. Then, identify the word by writing a *P* if the word is a possessive adjective or a *C* if the word is a contraction.

4. _____ The dog licked (its, it's) paw after stepping on a thorn.
5. _____ "(Your, You're) welcome to stay as long as you want," the gallery owner told us.
6. _____ Dave and Maria brought (their, they're) new instruments to band practice.
7. _____ Can you please put (your, you're) plate in the sink when you are finished eating?
8. _____ "(Its, It's) going to rain, and I forgot my umbrella!" she wailed.
9. _____ (Their, They're) planning to visit you as soon as you send them your new address.

> **FACTOID:** The world's smallest frog species lives in New Guinea and is about the size of a housefly.

DAY 20

Literary Terms/Writing

Read each sentence. Write *F* if the sentence is written from the first-person point of view. Write *T* if the sentence is written from the third-person point of view.

10. _____ My mother and I went to the garden store to buy a lilac bush for the backyard.

11. _____ Cal tapped her foot impatiently as she waited for her brother to finish getting ready.

12. _____ The hikers reached the summit of the hill just in time to see the sunrise.

13. _____ If you let me know what you like, then I will lend you any book from my library.

14. _____ The director was concerned that most of the people in the cast had never acted in a play before.

15. _____ Because he was afraid to fly, Leo had to travel across the country by train.

16. _____ When I have finished painting this landscape, I will begin a portrait of my cousin and his dog.

Madonna, a popular singer, said, "I think art should be controversial. I think it should make people think." Do you agree or disagree? Support your claim with reasons, opinions, and examples. Use another piece of paper if you need more space.

_____
_____
_____
_____
_____
_____

FITNESS FLASH: Hop on your left foot 5 times, then hop on your right foot 5 times.

* See page ii.

Science Experiment

BONUS

Changing the Melting Rate of Ice

What substances speed up the melting rate of ice?

The melting rate of ice is determined by how much thermal energy is needed to get the temperature of the ice to rise to its melting point. The melting point of ice can be changed when the water molecules interact with various chemicals.

In this activity, you will compare the melting rate of ice cubes that have been covered in different substances. You will determine which substances speed up the melting rate and, therefore, lower the melting point.

Materials:
- 5 cups
- 5 ice cubes
- stopwatch
- 1 Tbsp. sand
- 1 Tbsp. salt
- 1 Tbsp. sugar
- 1 Tbsp. baking soda

Procedure:
1. Place one ice cube in each of the five cups. Label the first cup "control" and set it aside. Label the other four cups with the name of one of the substances you will be experimenting with.
2. Carefully pour one tablespoon of each substance (sand, salt, sugar, and baking soda) onto the ice cube in the corresponding cup. Be sure to cover the ice cube with the substance.
3. Start the stopwatch and record how long it takes for each ice cube to melt. Record these times in the melting rate column of the table below.
4. Compare the melting rates of each of the ice cubes. Which substance or substances sped up the melting rate compared to the control?

Substance Covering the Ice Cube	Melting Rate (in minutes)
None (Control)	
Baking soda	
Salt	
Sand	
Sugar	

5. Use your data to explain why cities put salt on icy roads and sidewalks.

_____

_____

Science Experiment

BONUS

Chemical Reactions: Oxidation

When two substances react, sometimes the chemical reaction that occurs is visible. For example, when certain metals undergo a process called oxidation, they change color as they react with oxygen. One example of this is the Statue of Liberty, which is made of copper and was originally bronze in color. Over time, as the statue has been exposed to weather and the elements, it has turned green.

In this experiment, you will combine copper pennies with vinegar and salt, and observe oxidation in real time.

Materials:
- 2 or more pennies (pennies made before 1982, if possible)
- vinegar
- table salt
- 2 containers, such as bowls or paper cups
- paper towels

Procedure:

First, write down your observations about the pennies. What is their appearance like before you start the experiment?

_____

_____

In the first container, put a paper towel in the bottom and set at least one penny on top of it. Pour in vinegar until the penny is covered. In the second container, put a paper towel in the bottom and set at least one penny on top of it. Over this second penny, pour vinegar to cover and add a teaspoon of salt. Let the pennies sit for several hours.
What do you observe about the pennies after some time has passed?

_____

_____

Oxidation is a process in which an element, such as copper, loses electrons to the element oxygen. How do we know oxidation is occurring during the vinegar and penny reaction?

_____

_____

What other examples of oxidation can you think of that occur in daily life?

_____

_____

Social Studies Activity

BONUS

Read the passage. Then, create a timeline showing at least seven events in the life of Benjamin Franklin.

The Life of Benjamin Franklin

Benjamin Franklin, who is featured on the one-hundred-dollar bill, is one of the most remarkable figures in American history. Born in 1706 in Boston, he was the tenth of 17 children to a soap and candle maker. After his schooling ended at age 10, Franklin began learning the trade of printing as an apprentice to his brother. In 1723, he became a master printer and moved to Philadelphia and then London. In 1726, he crossed the Atlantic and returned to Philadelphia.

In 1728, Franklin established his own printing business. He then began to publish his own newspaper, the *Pennsylvania Gazette*. The success of this newspaper was followed by the highly popular *Poor Richard's Almanac*, which Franklin printed from 1732 to 1757. By 1748, Franklin had earned enough money to retire, but he still remained highly active in politics and in science.

One of the areas in which Franklin made major contributions was in the study of electricity. Starting in 1746, he began conducting experiments, which he described in his 1751 publication *Experiments and Observations on Electricity*. This work went through multiple editions. Afterward, he even experimented with electricity by flying a kite into a thunderstorm, something he became famous for. During this period, he was also credited with numerous inventions, including a battery, the lightning rod, bifocal eyeglasses, the Franklin stove, and even swim fins.

It could be argued, however, that Franklin's greatest contributions to society were political. Early on, he saw the need for the British colonies to unite. After the outbreak of the War of Independence (the Revolutionary War), he served as a member of Pennsylvania's delegation to the Constitutional Convention from 1775 to 1776. He also helped draft the Declaration of Independence in 1776. Because of his intelligence and charisma, Franklin was sent to the court of France, where he negotiated important military and political alliances that led to the end of the war. He was even one of the negotiators of the Treaty of Paris, which recognized American independence in 1783. In Franklin's last years, he served as the governor of Pennsylvania, and he signed the Constitution, the law the United States still follows today. In 1790, Benjamin Franklin died. He remains one of the most accomplished American citizens in the country's history.

BONUS

Social Studies Activity

Translating the Bill of Rights

The first ten Amendments to the U.S. Constitution are called the Bill of Rights. These amendments provide important protections for American citizens and help to support a democratic society. Sometimes these amendments are hard to understand because of the way they were written centuries ago. In this activity, read the amendments of the Bill of Rights. Then, in the space provided, summarize the meaning of each amendment using plain language.

1. **First Amendment**
   Congress shall make no law respecting an establishment of religion, or prohibiting the free exercise thereof; or abridging the freedom of speech, or of the press; or the right of the people peaceably to assemble, and to petition the Government for a redress of grievances.

   _____
   _____
   _____

2. **Second Amendment**
   A well regulated Militia, being necessary to the security of a free State, the right of the people to keep and bear Arms shall not be infringed.

   _____
   _____
   _____

3. **Third Amendment**
   No Soldier shall, in time of peace be quartered in any house, without the consent of the Owner, nor in time of war, but in a manner to be prescribed by law.

   _____
   _____
   _____

4. **Fourth Amendment**
   The right of the people to be secure in their persons, houses, papers, and effects, against unreasonable searches and seizures, shall not be violated, and no Warrants shall issue, but upon probable cause, supported by Oath or affirmation, and particularly describing the place to be searched, and the persons or things to be seized.

   _____
   _____
   _____
   _____

Social Studies Activity

BONUS

Use Your Navigational Skills with Latitude and Longitude

On a globe you will see imaginary lines called *longitude* and *latitude* that geographers use to determine position. The lines running from north to south are lines of longitude, starting with 0° at the prime meridian. These numbers grow either east or west until they reach 180° at the other side of the world at the International Date Line. The lines running east to west are lines of latitude. The equator is 0° latitude, with the numbers getting larger until they reach 90° at the North Pole and the South Pole. The expression of a location's longitude and latitude is called its *coordinate*.

Use an atlas or a globe to locate a major city near each of these coordinates (rounded to the nearest degree). Write the name of the city in the space provided. Then write the coordinates of cities listed below.

	City	Latitude	Longitude
1.	_____	34°N	84°W
2.	_____	44°N	79°W
3.	_____	40°N	4°E
4.	_____	40°N	116°E
5.	_____	34°S	151°E
6.	_____	34°N	118°W
7.	_____	15°N	121°E
8.	_____	34°S	18°E

	City	Latitude	Longitude
9.	Buenos Aires, Argentina	_____	_____
10.	Cairo, Egypt	_____	_____
11.	Ulaanbaatar, Mongolia	_____	_____
12.	Chicago, Illinois	_____	_____
13.	Wellington, New Zealand	_____	_____
14.	St. Petersburg, Russia	_____	_____
15.	Addis Ababa, Ethiopia	_____	_____
16.	Havana, Cuba	_____	_____

Outdoor Extension Activities

BONUS

Take it Outside!

Here are three ideas for things you can do this summer to spend more time outdoors:

Make an outdoor must-do list. Write at least five things on your list that you would like to do outdoors this summer. Be creative! Take a picture of yourself completing each thing on your list. Share your list and your photos with your friends and family.

Find an outdoor restaurant or café in your area. With a family member, attend this restaurant for a meal outdoors, al fresco. Bring a pen and a notebook and act like a food critic. Use descriptive language and your senses. Take notes about your experience during the meal. Afterward, read your notes and write a review of the restaurant. Share your review with family members who joined you.

Create a scavenger hunt of things to find around your neighborhood while walking or biking. Make a list of 5–10 things to find. This can include things like garden statues, flags, or unique decorations. You can also include more generic things on your list, such as:

- a house address ending in an odd number
- a street name with more than eight letters
- a yellow house or building
- a red car
- a squirrel
- a person walking a dog

Find a friend to complete your scavenger hunt. Encourage your friend to develop a similar scavenger hunt for you to complete around your neighborhood.

© Carson Dellosa Education

SECTION II

Monthly Goals

Think of three goals to set for yourself this month. For example, you may want to read for 30 minutes each day. Write your goals on the lines. Post them somewhere that you will see them every day.

Draw a check mark beside each goal you meet. Feel proud that you have met your goals and continue to set new ones to challenge yourself.

1. _____
2. _____
3. _____

Word List

The following words are used in this section. Use a dictionary to look up each word that you do not know. Then, write three sentences. Use at least one word from the word list in each sentence.

abate
clutter
evasive
grievance
irrefutable

lament
obstinate
temperate
zeal

1. _____
_____
2. _____
_____
3. _____
_____

FITNESS FLASH: Do 15 windmills.

* See page ii.

SECTION II

Introduction to Strength

This section includes fitness and character development activities that focus on strength. These activities are designed to get you moving and thinking about strengthening your body and your character.

Physical Strength

Like flexibility, strength is important for a healthy body. Many people think that a strong person is someone who can lift an enormous amount of weight. However, strength is more than the ability to pick up heavy barbells. Having strength is important for many everyday activities, such as helping with yardwork or helping a younger sibling get into a car. Muscular strength also helps reduce stress on your joints as your body ages. Everyday activities and many fun exercises provide opportunities for you to build strength. Carrying bags of groceries, riding a bicycle, and swimming are all excellent ways to strengthen your muscles. Classic exercises, such as push-ups and chin-ups, are also fantastic strength-builders.

Set realistic, achievable goals to improve your strength based on the activities that you enjoy. Evaluate your progress during the summer months and set new strength goals for yourself as you accomplish your previous goals.

Strength of Character

As you build your physical strength, work on your inner strength as well. Having a strong character means standing up for your beliefs, even if others do not agree with your viewpoint. Inner strength can be shown in many ways. For example, you can show inner strength by being honest, standing up for someone who needs your help, and putting your best effort into every task. It is not always easy to show inner strength. Think of a time when you showed inner strength, such as telling the truth when you broke your mother's favorite vase. How did you use your inner strength to handle that situation? Use the summer months to develop a strong sense of self, both physically and emotionally. Celebrate your successes and look for ways to become even stronger. Reflect upon your accomplishments during the summer, and you will see positive growth on the inside and on the outside.

Algebra/Grammar

DAY 1

Simplify each compound inequality.

1. $8x - 5 > 11$ and $9x + 1 < 82$ _____
2. $46 + 7c \leq 67$ or $10 \geq 2c$ _____
3. $19 \leq 4d - 1 \leq 47$ _____
4. $6t \geq 2t + 4$ and $t + 5 \geq 2$ _____
5. $10g < -200$ or $5 < 40 + 5g$ _____
6. $35 < 2 + 11z < 112$ _____

A semicolon can be used to join two independent clauses to form one compound sentence. Semicolons should be used to join sentences whose ideas are related. Combine the two sentences using a semicolon. Write the new sentence on the line below. Then, write two original compound sentences that include a semicolon.

7. Julia is playing volleyball again. She is learning many new skills.
   _____

8. The students refused to do their homework. They said it was too difficult.
   _____

9. It was rush hour. The city streets were filled with people hurrying to catch their trains home.
   _____

10. Ryan practices the violin for three hours each day. He is a focused and talented musician.
    _____

11. Walking is a great form of exercise. It strengthens your muscles and improves your circulation.
    _____

12. _____

13. _____

CHARACTER CHECK: What is something you can do to show respect for yourself?

DAY 1

Vocabulary/Science

Underline the two words that are antonyms in each sentence.

14. Ella cluttered the table with materials for her art project, but she tidied up before her parents got home.
15. The author would allow small changes to be made to her story, but she did not want any drastic changes to be made when turning her book into a movie.
16. Amy's idea for a family vacation was met with zeal from her younger daughter and disinterest from her older son.
17. When writing to persuade, using concise sentences can be more effective than using long ones.

Write the words from the word bank on the correct lines.

cell wall   vacuole   cytoplasm   ribosome
chloroplast   mitochondria   nucleus   Golgi body

Plant Cell

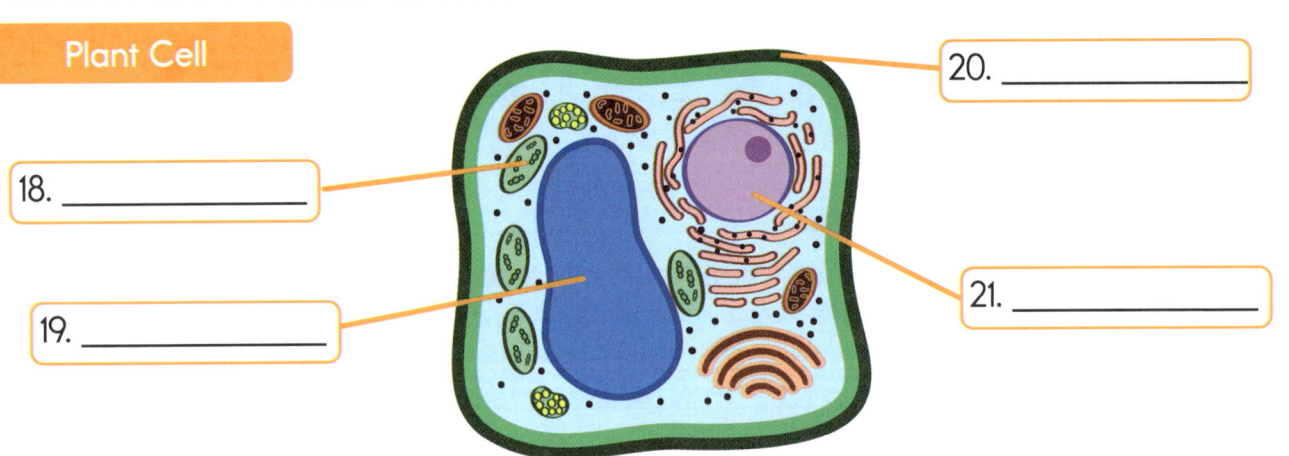

18. _____
19. _____
20. _____
21. _____

Animal Cell

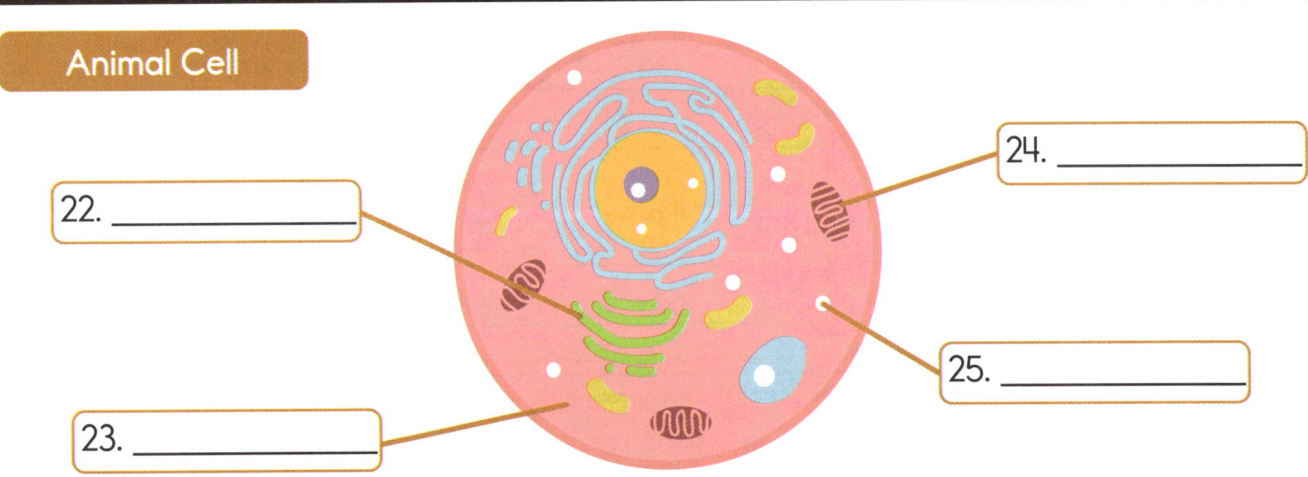

22. _____
23. _____
24. _____
25. _____

Algebra/Parts of Speech

DAY 2

In each of the following equations, solve for the indicated variable.

1. $s = \dfrac{d}{t}$; $t =$ _____
2. $F = ma$; $m =$ _____
3. $\dfrac{v - u}{t} = a$; $v =$ _____
4. $q - 1 = 2p^2$; $p =$ _____
5. $Ax + By = C$; $y =$ _____
6. $a^2 + b^2 = c^2$; $a =$ _____
7. $E = mc^2$; $m =$ _____
8. $\dfrac{2(b - a)}{c} = d$; $b =$ _____

An *adjective* is a word that describes a noun. Adjectives can add information about things like quantity, value, size, temperature, age, shape, or color. An adjective usually appears before the noun that it is describing. Rewrite each sentence and add an adjective to make it more descriptive. Underline your adjective.

9. Renee ate a piece of watermelon at the picnic.
   _____

10. The dinner table was big enough for all five guests.
    _____

11. Dante's brother rolled around in the grass.
    _____

12. When the rabbit heard us coming, it hopped back into the woods.
    _____

13. I looked out my window and saw that the ground was covered in snow.
    _____

14. Mia wore a dress to the graduation ceremony.
    _____

FACTOID: Angel Falls in Venezuela is the world's tallest waterfall on land at more than 3,200 feet tall.

DAY 2

Reading Comprehension

Read the passage. Then, answer the questions.

The Legend of Sundiata, King of Mali

According to history, the great King Sundiata of Mali was born in 1235. He established Mali as a center for trade that extended through much of Africa and the Arab world, making his country one of the world's richest empires. His empire was also one of the first to protect human rights, advocating for the **abolition** of slavery and the spread of education. Facts about Sundiata's life can be found in the historical record, but another account of his life may be better known: the legend of Sundiata, the Lion King.

This legend has been told for hundreds of years and begins at the court of Sundiata's father, Maghan Kon Fatta. Before Sundiata was born, two hunters came to Maghan's court and told him that he would have a son who would be the most powerful king in the world. Maghan already had a wife and a son, Dankaran, but the hunters told him that this special son would have to be born to a second wife. So he married again. When Sundiata was born, his legs were deformed; he was unable to walk. One day, though, Sundiata found magical iron rods that helped him stand up, and his strength was so great that he was able to lift up a tree by its roots and give it to his mother.

After Maghan's death, Dankaran became king, and Sundiata was forced out of the kingdom. Dankaran was a weak king, and Mali was eventually overtaken by Soumaoro Kanté, the king of the neighboring empire of Sosso. In his exile, Sundiata heard of the troubles in his homeland. He raised an army and returned, defeating Soumaoro and becoming king of Mali. He ruled over a period of great peace and prosperity and became known as the Lion King.

15. Which best summarizes the main idea of this passage?
    A. Sundiata was a weak ruler, and Mali was overtaken during his reign.
    B. Sundiata overcame obstacles in his childhood to become a great king.
    C. Sundiata is a historical figure who is also the subject of a popular legend.
    D. Sundiata brought wealth to Mali by advancing trade and protecting human rights.

16. Which of the following best defines the word *abolition*?
    A. criticizing
    B. ending
    C. forgetting
    D. spreading

17. Which sentence from the passage is an opinion?
    A. His empire was also one of the first to protect human rights.
    B. This legend has been told for hundreds of years.
    C. Dankaran was a weak king.
    D. He raised an army and returned, defeating Soumaoro.

Algebra/Vocabulary

DAY 3

Write the coordinate of the *y*-intercept for each graph.

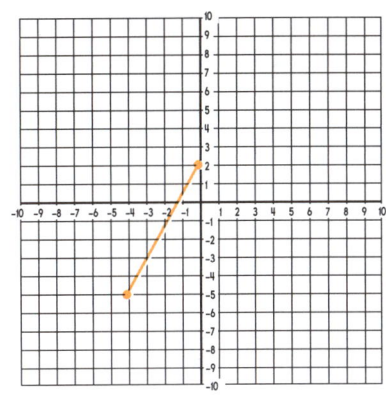 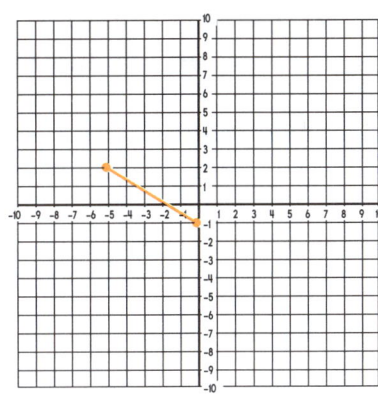 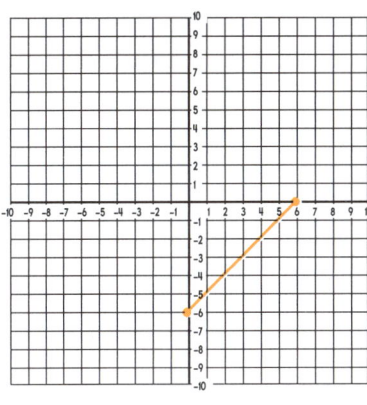

1. _____ 2. _____ 3. _____

Write the coordinate of the *y*-intercept of each equation.

4. $y = 2x - 3$

5. $2x + 4y = 8$

6. $-5x - 3y = 30$

_____   _____   _____

Match each root word in the first column with its meaning in the second column. Use a dictionary if you need help.

7. *vac* as in *vacancy*   two
8. *juven* as in *juvenile*   water
9. *trans* as in *transit*   foot
10. *lumin* as in *luminous*   under
11. *aqua* as in *aquatic*   outside normal events
12. *amphi* as in *amphibious*   light
13. *ped* as in *pedestrian*   empty
14. *bi* as in *binoculars*   of both kinds
15. *sub* as in *subordinate*   a youthful person
16. *extra* as in *extraordinary*   across or through

CHARACTER CHECK: Write about a time that you showed respect for another person.

DAY 3

Vocabulary/Algebra

Look up each word in an online or print dictionary. Circle the syllable that is stressed. Then, write the word's part of speech and definition on the line. If the word has more than one definition and part of speech, then use the first one listed.

17. abate _____

18. lament _____

19. deliberate _____

20. ornate _____

21. pilfer _____

The slope of a line is its rate of change. Use the two given points, (x_1, y_1) and (x_2, y_2), and the equation $m = \dfrac{y_2 - y_1}{x_2 - x_1}$ to find the slope, m, of the given lines.

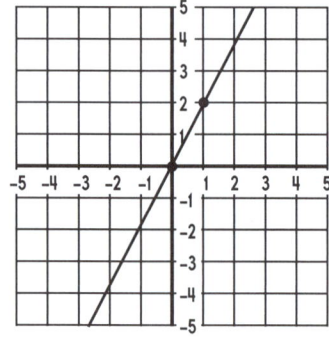
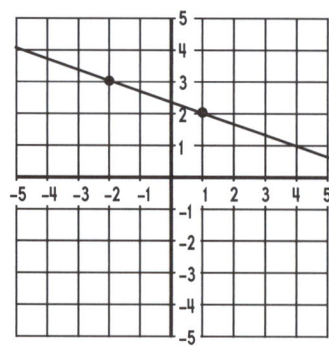
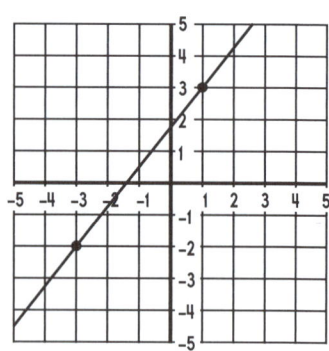

22. $m = $ _____

23. $m = $ _____

24. $m = $ _____

CHARACTER CHECK: Draw a comic strip showing a character who demonstrates perseverance.

Writing/Grammar

DAY 4

Imagine you are walking at a park one day and you find a key beneath some leaves. You ask around and the key does not belong to anyone. What do you think the key opens? Write a story describing what the key unlocks and how you discover this. Use another piece of paper if you need more space.

_____
_____
_____
_____
_____
_____
_____
_____
_____
_____

Circle the verb that correctly completes each sentence.

1. Kai (stays, stayed) after school yesterday for his chess club meeting.
2. The restaurant (closes, closed) at nine o'clock last week.
3. The rain (was starting, will start) tomorrow morning before sunrise.
4. The package (was delivered, will be delivered) to my neighbor's house by mistake.
5. Leo (has been playing, was playing) soccer since he was three years old.
6. While Abby was riding the train to work, she (falls, fell) asleep.
7. Grand Teton National Park (is, are) located in Wyoming.
8. Doing yoga can (improve, improved) flexibility and balance.

FACTOID: There are 256 tablespoons in 1 gallon.

DAY 4

Vocabulary/Fitness

Circle the word that correctly completes each analogy.

9. *Polar* is to *cold* as *temperate* is to _____.
   A. mild B. hot
   C. dry D. rainy

10. *Abbreviate* is to *lengthen* as *contaminate* is to _____.
    A. clean B. infect
    C. forget D. join

11. *Dislike* is to *loathe* as *like* is to _____.
    A. hate B. adore
    C. tolerate D. forgive

12. *Orphan* is to *family* as *nomad* is to _____.
    A. animals B. money
    C. profession D. home

13. *Superior* is to *above* as *subordinate* is to _____.
    A. after B. beside
    C. under D. before

14. *Dissatisfied* is to *unhappy* as *conspicuous* is to _____.
    A. hostile B. visible
    C. secret D. agreeable

15. *Democracy* is to *president* as *monarchy* is to _____.
    A. senate B. king
    C. election D. dictator

16. *Evasive* is to *directness* as *aloof* is to _____.
    A. distance B. friendliness
    C. concern D. responsibility

Stretching

Stretching is the best way to warm up your muscles and keep them strong and flexible. It also helps to prevent injuries.

Start with stretching your arms high over your head. Lift your arms as high above your head as you can. Stretch your fingertips toward the sky. Hold this position for 10 seconds. Sit on the floor with your legs folded in and the soles of your feet touching. Imagine your folded legs are butterfly wings and flutter your legs up and down 20 times while holding your feet together. Finally, while sitting on the floor, stretch your legs out to the sides, forming a V. Lean your body over to rest your arms and head on your right knee for 10 seconds. Repeat by leaning over your left knee.

Simple stretches like these are a great way to keep your body happy and healthy.

Algebra/Grammar

DAY 5

Find the slope of each line by using the coordinates of points on the line.

1. (−1, −2) and (−1, 2) _____
2. (0, −3) and (4, 1) _____
3. (−1, 3) and (1, −5) _____
4. (−2, 5) and (−1, 2) _____
5. (−1, −2) and (0, 2) _____
6. (1, 3) and (2, 2) _____
7. (2, 5) and (−1, 2) _____
8. (−1, 2) and (0, 2) _____

Read the paragraph. Correct the punctuation and correct any other errors as necessary.

I recently visited the metropolitan museum of art in New York City. While I expected the museum to be filled with works of art like painting and sculpture I did not expect it to contain so many historical artifacts. The museums Egyptian wing for example has an amazing collection of mummies. I also saw jewelry and household objects like bowls and perfume bottles that the ancient Egyptians used the exhibit even contained an actual Egyptian temple the Temple of Dendur which was built over two thousand years ago. Another fascinating glimpse into the past was the arms and armor exhibit I saw suits of armor worn by people (and horses!) throughout history and around the world and the museum even had a suit of armor worn by King Henry the VIII of England. For me, the museum really made history come alive!

FACTOID: Did you know that fish can cough?

Reading Comprehension

DAY 5

Read the passage. Then, answer the questions.

The Mars Rovers

Mars has been explored by many NASA missions, including some that have used orbiters, landers, and rovers. Currently, there are five rovers on Mars, two of which are still in operation. A rover is a motor vehicle that can move around on wheels and help scientists gather data about the planet. The rovers on Mars include Sojourner, Spirit, Opportunity, Curiosity, and Perseverance. Sojourner landed in 1997; and the newest rover, Perseverance, landed in early 2021.

Each rover has provided astronomers and engineers with new information about Mars. Rovers send pictures to Earth, take rock samples, study weather and temperatures, and explore land features of the surface of Mars. Sojourner was the first rover to land on Mars and was quite small, just about the size of a microwave oven. Spirit and Opportunity (2004) were sent together and are twin rovers with identical features. Curiosity (2012) is the largest rover sent to Mars.

Perseverance is unique in that it brought along a partner helicopter, Ingenuity. Ingenuity is the first vehicle to take flight from the surface of Mars. Taking flight on Mars is quite a challenge due to the very low level of available atmospheric gas, which makes it difficult to achieve the force of lift against air molecules that allows a vehicle to take off. The main goal of the latest rover, Perseverance, is to study the Jezero Crater for signs of life. The rover is looking for evidence of microbial remains. It is also running tests to see if oxygen can be extracted from the air (which contains mostly carbon dioxide gas) to be used by future human missions to Mars.

9. What is the name of the first rover to land on Mars?
   A. Curiosity
   B. Perseverance
   C. Sojourner
   D. Spirit

10. Which best describes the main goal of the Perseverance rover?
    A. to study the land features and weather on Mars
    B. to look for signs of life near the Jezero Crater
    C. to measure temperatures of the rocks on Mars
    D. to send pictures of Mars back to Earth

11. Which two rovers were identical in their construction? (Choose two.)
    A. Curiosity
    B. Opportunity
    C. Perseverance
    D. Spirit

12. Explain why it is difficult for an aircraft to take flight from the surface of Mars.

_____

_____

Algebra/Language Arts

DAY 6

Determine whether each equation represents a *linear function* or a *nonlinear function*. Write your answer on the line.

1. $y = -6x + 10$ _____
2. $y = 0.3(x - 25)$ _____
3. $y = x^2 - 9x - 30$ _____
4. $y = 148 + 21x$ _____
5. $y = -17x^4 - 1$ _____
6. $y = -28x$ _____

A *simile* is a comparison of two unlike things using *like* or *as*. A *metaphor* is an implied comparison of two unlike things without using *like* or *as*. Underline the simile or metaphor in each sentence. Write an *S* on the line if the sentence contains a simile. Write an *M* on the line if the sentence contains a metaphor.

7. _____ The moon was a beacon that the weary sailors followed home.

8. _____ Time is a river that flows in only one direction.

9. _____ The heated blanket was like a warm hug around me.

10. _____ The soft sound of the wind was a whisper in my ear.

11. _____ The new kitten's fur is as soft as velvet.

12. _____ Ms. Marino's suggestion was like a seed planted in my mind.

Write a sentence of your own that includes a simile. Underline the simile.

_____

Write a sentence of your own that includes a metaphor. Underline the metaphor.

_____

FITNESS FLASH: March in place for 30 seconds with high knee lifts.

* See page ii.

DAY 6

Vocabulary/Writing

Read each word. Write the root word and the suffix for each word in the correct column.

	Root Word	Suffix
13. automation	_____	_____
14. harmonize	_____	_____
15. disreputable	_____	_____
16. comparative	_____	_____
17. invigorating	_____	_____
18. grievance	_____	_____
19. displacement	_____	_____
20. dispensable	_____	_____
21. defensive	_____	_____
22. custodian	_____	_____

Do you think there should be a student uniform enforced by schools, or should students be allowed to wear whatever they want? Choose a side and then write a persuasive argument justifying your reasoning.

_____
_____
_____
_____
_____
_____

Percentages

DAY 7

Solve each problem.

1. Luis works at an ice cream shop. Today, he served 13 scoops of chocolate ice cream, 8 scoops of vanilla ice cream, and 21 scoops of strawberry ice cream. What percentage of scoops today were chocolate? Round your answer to the nearest percent.

   _____

2. Gabrielle sees a 30% discount on potted plants at the nursery. She chooses 3 potted plants whose regular prices are $3.59, $4.25, and $3.99. What is the total she will pay after the discount? Round your answer to the nearest cent and do not include sales tax.

   _____

3. Camilla learned that about 15% of the birds at the bird refuge are finches. She also reads on a sign that the bird refuge has tracked about 140 finches living there. What is the approximate total bird population? Round your answer to the nearest whole number.

   _____

4. Ali gave the waiter an 18% tip after his meal, and he paid a total of $17.23. What was the cost of his meal before the tip? Round your answer to the nearest cent.

   _____

5. Mariam puts $450 in a savings account that earns 2% interest per year, compounded yearly. If she leaves the money and interest in the account for 3 years, then what will the total amount be? Round your answer to the nearest cent.

   _____

6. A bar of dark chocolate is advertised to contain 60% pure cocoa. The total weight of the bar is 8 ounces. How many ounces of the bar are pure cocoa?

   _____

7. Ying's net pay is $1,560. He pays 25% of his gross income for taxes and also has 3% of his gross income taken out to go toward retirement savings. What is his gross income? Round your answer to the nearest cent.

   _____

8. A stadium with 2,000 seats is filled with 1,300 people. What is the attendance of the stadium, as a percent of capacity?

   _____

DAY 7

Data Analysis/Critical Thinking

Determine the relative frequency of each. Write the relative frequency as a decimal.

9. The table below shows how many students in Mr. Wolff's class play each instrument. What is the relative frequency of students who play the drums?

Instrument	Number of Students
flute	6
clarinet	8
trumpet	3
drums	3
saxophone	5

_____

10. In a class of 20 students, 7 are girls. What is the relative frequency of the number of girls?

_____

11. A coin is flipped 10 times. The result of each flip is shown, with H for heads and T for tails:
H T T T T H H H T H T
What is the relative frequency of landing on heads?

_____

Several friends all have different types of pets: a bird, a cat, a frog, a rabbit, and a snake. Use the information and deductive reasoning to determine which pet belongs to each friend.

- Jayden's pet is a reptile.
- Both Aisha's pet and Jake's pet have four legs.
- Kym's pet is not a mammal.
- Tierra's pet has a short, fluffy tail.
- Aisha's pet is an amphibian.

	bird	cat	frog	rabbit	snake
Aisha					
Jake					
Jayden					
Kym					
Tierra					

Problem Solving/Grammar

DAY 8

Solve each problem.

1. A teacher gives a test with 15 questions that is worth 35 points. It includes multiple choice questions, worth 1 point each, and short response questions, worth 5 points each. How many multiple-choice and short response questions are on the test?
   _____ multiple choice
   _____ short response

2. A baker makes cakes and pies. She uses 1 cup of flour for each cake and $\frac{3}{4}$ cup of flour for each pie. In total, she made 14 desserts and used $11\frac{3}{4}$ cups of flour. How many pies and cakes did she make?
   _____ cakes
   _____ pies

3. Tickets to the zoo cost $25 per adult and $10 per child. A group of 12 people pay $180 for tickets to this zoo. How many adults and how many children were in the group?
   _____ adults
   _____ children

An *appositive* is a noun, a pronoun, or a noun phrase that usually follows another noun or pronoun and describes it. The appositive is set off by commas. A *main clause* has a subject and a verb, and it expresses a complete thought. A *subordinate clause* has a subject and a verb but does not express a complete thought.

Read the pair of sentences.

Alex is an excellent public speaker. Alex won first place at the debate competition.

4. Combine the pair of sentences so that the new sentence has an appositive. Underline the appositive. _____

5. Combine the pair of sentences so that the new sentence has a main clause and a subordinate clause. Underline the subordinate clause. _____

DAY 8

Reading Comprehension

Read the passage. Then, answer the questions.

Diwali: The Festival of Lights

In the Hindu, Jain, and Sikh faiths, one of the most important celebrations is Diwali. This five-day festival, which usually takes place in October or November, is known as the "Festival of Lights" and is a general celebration of the forces of good over evil. As such, a common mark of the festival is the lighting of small oil lamps called *diyas*. These are used to decorate homes and streets, and are even floated along rivers. During Diwali, families and friends visit one another and exchange gifts. Other traditions include feasting and performing acts of piety. Gambling is permitted and encouraged during Diwali as a way of bringing good fortune for the upcoming year. Children enjoy Diwali for the firework displays and the sweets.

Diwali is also an incredibly diverse holiday that is celebrated differently by different religious groups. In Jainism, the holiday marks the enlightenment of one of the founders of the religion. The Sikh faith uses the holiday to celebrate the release from imprisonment of Guru Hargobind Singh. Hindus in various locales view the holiday as a celebration of the birthday of Lakshmi, the goddess of wealth, or of her marriage to the god Vishnu. Different regions of South Asia also place different significance on Diwali. For example, many people in South Asia use Diwali to celebrate the defeat of the demon Narakasura by the god Krishna; in Bengal, celebrants honor the goddess Kali.

Each of the five days of Diwali has special significance. The first day is used to clean the home and buy small golden items. The second day often involves decorating homes with the clay lamps central to the celebration, as well as with floral artistic patterns called *rangoli*. The third day, which is the high point of Diwali, is marked by families getting together for prayer. This is followed by feasts and celebrations. The fourth day is the start of the New Year and is marked by visits from friends and relatives, who bring gifts. Finally, on the fifth day, the celebration winds down by honoring the relationship between brothers and sisters.

6. Why is Diwali considered a diverse holiday?
   A. It marks the start of the new year.
   B. It is celebrated over five days.
   C. It is held throughout South India.
   D. It is celebrated in different forms.

7. How is the third day of Diwali celebrated as a climax of the holiday? _____
_____

FITNESS FLASH: Do 10 mountain climbers, starting in a push-up position.

* See page ii.

Algebra/Parts of Speech

DAY 9

Find the value of the variable in each equation.

1. $4x = 12$

2. $\dfrac{y}{5} = 4$

3. $a + 14 = 25$

4. $10 - b = 3$

5. $40r = 8$

6. $d - 3 = -2$

A verb in the *indicative mood* expresses a fact or an opinion.
EXAMPLE: The sun will be setting soon.

A verb in the *imperative mood* expresses a command or a request.
EXAMPLE: Clean off your desk after you finish your project.

A verb in the *interrogative mood* asks a question.
EXAMPLE: How many students attended the rally?

A verb in the *conditional mood* expresses something that is dependent on a condition.
EXAMPLE: If I had known the answer, then I would have raised my hand.

Read each sentence. Identify the verb mood by writing *I* (indicative), *IM* (imperative), *IN* (interrogative), or *C* (conditional).

7. _____ We could clearly see the Big Dipper in the night sky.
8. _____ How old is the oldest Egyptian pyramid?
9. _____ If the house of cards had been sturdier, then it would not have fallen over.
10. _____ The gust of wind spun the blades of the pinwheel.
11. _____ Does anyone here know how to make a quilt?
12. _____ Make sure you sign up to help with the food drive.
13. _____ If Carson had bought enough tickets, then we all could have gone to the play.
14. _____ Will you plant an apple tree or a pear tree in your yard?
15. _____ My dog weighs almost 25 pounds.
16. _____ Please put this book back on the shelf after you read it.

DAY 9

Vocabulary/Character Development

Homophones are words that sound the same but have different meanings and spellings. Circle the letter next to the homophone that correctly completes each sentence.

17. Lucia grabbed the last _____ of her grandmother's homemade banana cream pie.
    A. piece
    B. peace

18. Prince Charles is the _____ to the throne in Great Britain.
    A. air
    B. heir

19. My voice was _____ after cheering my sister on at the basketball game last night.
    A. horse
    B. hoarse

20. "Ok, I hear you. I am awake," James said with a _____.
    A. groan
    B. grown

21. It is important to begin all proper nouns with a _____ letter.
    A. capital
    B. capitol

22. The _____ just retired after finishing his thirtieth year at the high school.
    A. principle
    B. principal

23. Helena went to the nurse after her friend told her that she looked _____.
    A. pale
    B. pail

24. Completing a triathlon is an amazing _____!
    A. feet
    B. feat

Empathy

Empathy is the ability to understand and share the feelings of another person.

25. First, think of a time where someone expressed empathy to you. What was the scenario? What did they do to express empathy?

    _____
    _____
    _____

26. Now, think of a time where you expressed empathy to someone you know. What was the scenario? What did you do to express empathy?

    _____
    _____
    _____

Functions/Parts of Speech

DAY 10

Write the equation of a line in slope-intercept form given the slope and y-intercept.

1. slope: 0.2; y-intercept: (0, −4)
   _____

2. slope: −5; y-intercept: (0, 38)
   _____

Write the equation of a line in slope-intercept form given the slope and a point on the line.

3. slope: 6; point: (2, 5)
   _____

4. slope: $\frac{3}{4}$; point: (16, −10)
   _____

Write the equation of a line in point-slope form given the slope and a point on the line.

5. slope: −3; point: (11, −8)
   _____

6. slope: $\frac{7}{10}$; point: (−3, 9)
   _____

A *gerund* is a verb form that is used as a noun and ends in *-ing*. Each sentence has two words ending in *-ing*. One of them is a gerund, and one is not. Circle the gerund in each sentence.

7. I find stamp collecting to be an interesting hobby.
8. Karl is hoping to be able to try cross-country skiing someday.
9. Baking five different batches of granola bars for the bake sale was challenging!
10. Practicing guitar in your garage is not working for me.
11. Listening to classical music is a very relaxing pastime.
12. Michaela is willing to help you with your gardening.
13. When the dog is sleeping, is it dreaming about cats and tennis balls?
14. Because our new neighbors were very welcoming, moving to our new house was a great experience.
15. Anne is thinking about planning her sister's surprise party next month.
16. Are you considering asking Coach Alvero for help with your fastball?

CHARACTER CHECK: What makes you feel confident about yourself?

DAY 10

Vocabulary/Science

Homonyms are words that sound the same and are spelled the same but have different meanings. Read each sentence and look at the underlined homonym. Decide which meaning of the homonym should be used.

17. The point of my pencil broke.
    - A. to show position
    - B. a sharp tip
    - C. a reason for something
    - D. exact position; a dot

18. With one quick hop, Matt will scale the fence.
    - A. an object used to measure mass
    - B. an animal covering
    - C. a series of marks at certain intervals
    - D. to climb something

19. The park ranger used a match to light the campfire.
    - A. an equivalent pair
    - B. a flammable material
    - C. a sports event
    - D. to fit together

Read the following passage about types of rocks and review the word bank. Write the letter of the word from the word bank that correctly completes each sentence. Use the internet for help if needed.

A. igneous	B. metamorphic	C. sedimentary	D. layered
E. crumbled	F. hard	G. foliated	H. non-foliated
I. intrusive	J. extrusive		

There are three classes of rocks.

The first class, called _____, is formed when sediments are compacted. This class of rocks is distinctly _____. They are also easily _____.

The second class of rocks is _____. This class is formed through the solidification of magma or lava. There are two types: _____, which is formed through the rapid cooling of lava, and _____, which is formed through the slow cooling of magma. This class of rocks is known for being _____.

The third class is _____, which is formed through the transformation of older rocks. It is a sort of mix between the first two classes, with variety in hardness and layering. As such, it is sorted into two types: _____, which has layers, and _____, which does not have layers.

Ratios/Literary Terms

DAY 11

Calculate the unit rate for each situation described. Round to the nearest hundredth. Then, compare the unit rates by circling the word that correctly completes the sentence.

1. At the fair, Juanito ate 7 hot dogs in $2\frac{1}{2}$ minutes. Juanito's unit rate: _____

   Gerry ate $17\frac{3}{4}$ hot dogs in 6 minutes. Gerry's unit rate: _____

   Juanito ate (more / fewer) hot dogs per minute than Gerry.

2. Kia rode her bike for 50 minutes and went 8 miles. Kia's unit rate: _____

   Mo rode 12.5 miles in 1 hour and 15 minutes. Mo's unit rate: _____

   Kia rode (faster / slower) than Mo.

3. Antonio rode in Taxi A and paid $35.10 for a 10.8-mile ride.

   Taxi A's unit rate: _____

   Omar rode in Taxi B and paid $12.72 for a 3.18-mile ride.

   Taxi B's unit rate: _____

   Taxi A costs (more / less) per mile than Taxi B.

Write the letter of the word from the word bank that matches each description.

> A. simile   B. metaphor   C. alliteration   D. idiom
> E. personification   F. hyperbole   G. onomatopoeia

4. _____ He was as hungry as a horse.
5. _____ The trees danced in the wind.
6. _____ The fluttering fairies flew in the forest.
7. _____ The wasp buzzed angrily as it flew over my head.
8. _____ Tony is a statue as he stands waiting.
9. _____ It was raining cats and dogs outside last night.
10. _____ That test seemed to take a million hours to finish.

FACTOID: Sharks have no bones in their bodies.

DAY 11

Reading Comprehension

Read the passage. Then, answer the questions.

Marvelous Maltese

Are you a dog lover? What is your favorite breed? Do you like big dogs, small dogs, or something in between? If you are looking for the perfect pup to bring into your home, then look no further than the Maltese breed.

A Maltese is a type of small dog that weighs 10 pounds or less and typically has a height of 10 inches or less. This breed is **hypoallergenic**, which means Maltese do not shed and should not cause people to have allergic reactions. Maltese are known for their straight, silky white coats and their large dark eyes.

One advantage of owning a Maltese dog is that it will likely have a long life span—approximately 12–15 years. Another advantage is that this type of dog is known for being an excellent companion that loves being around people. Many Maltese also serve as therapy dogs. Also, these dogs are intelligent and typically easy to train, though they have a penchant for stubbornness. Maltese love attention and greeting visitors. They are friendly with other dogs, as well.

One possible disadvantage to owning Maltese dogs is that they are protective of their home and often act as watchdogs. They are prone to frequent barking, which can be tiresome. There are harm-free training methods that can be used to help curb incessant barking. Because of their small size, Maltese dogs are not recommended for families with very young children.

Overall, if you are looking for a small, friendly breed of dog that enjoys playtime, as well as relaxing in your lap, then the Maltese may be the perfect pet for you.

11. A Maltese is best suited for which type of family?
    A. a family with two toddlers and another dog
    B. a family looking for a large dog that does not like to play or run
    C. a family living in a small apartment building that does not allow pets
    D. a family living in a townhouse with a seven-year-old

12. What does it mean if a dog is hypoallergenic?
    A. It means the dog does not have food allergies.
    B. It means the dog does not shed.
    C. It means the dog is extremely allergenic.
    D. It means the dog likes being in water.

13. Do you have a dog? If so, then describe what kind of dog you have. If you do not have a dog, then explain which type of dog or other pet you would like if you were able to get one.

_____

_____

Geometry/Parts of Speech

DAY 12

In each problem below, the coordinates for pre-image ABCD are given, along with a transformation or sequence of transformations. Give the coordinates of the image A'B'C'D' after the transformation(s).

If you get stuck, then try graphing the pre-image ABCD on a separate piece of paper. Then, apply the transformation(s) to the graph to find the image coordinates.

1. A: (–1, 3), B: (2, 5), C: (6, 0), D: (0, 0); Translate left 2 units and down 5 units.

   A': _____   B': _____   C': _____   D': _____

2. A: (4, 4), B: (9, –8), C: (4, –4), D: (2, 0); Reflect across the y-axis.

   A': _____   B': _____   C': _____   D': _____

3. A: (–6, –1), B: (–6, –6), C: (0, –6), D: (0, 2); Rotate 90° counterclockwise about the origin.

   A': _____   B': _____   C': _____   D': _____

4. A: (–10, 3), B: (–8, 6), C: (2, 2), D: (4, –2); Translate right 1 unit and up 6 units, then reflect across the x-axis.

   A': _____   B': _____   C': _____   D': _____

Correlative conjunctions are word pairs that join similar words, phrases, or clauses. Correlative conjunctions include *both/and, neither/nor, whether/or, either/or,* and *not only/but* (or *but also*). Write the appropriate correlative conjunctions to complete each sentence.

5. The students should decide _____ they want to take Spanish _____ French next year.

6. You will not be able to swim in the pool if you have _____ a swimsuit _____ a swimming cap.

7. If you are planning to go camping, then you should bring _____ food to cook _____ water to drink.

8. The tour group _____ visited the Statue of Liberty _____ was able to climb to the viewing platform in her crown.

9. _____ the principal _____ the vice principal was able to answer the question about the bake sale.

DAY 12

Reading Comprehension

Read the passage. Then, answer the questions.

The Great Salt Lake Is Shrinking

After the Great Lakes, the Great Salt Lake in Utah is the largest body of water within the United States. Unlike the Great Lakes, the Great Salt Lake is, like its name suggests, salty. It is about four times saltier than the ocean. This is because the lake is a terminal lake, which means that it is a body of water into which water flows and stays. The water then evaporates, but it leaves salt behind. Thus, over very long periods of time, the water becomes saltier and saltier. This is particularly true of the Great Salt Lake, since it is in a very arid environment, which promotes evaporation. In this way, the Great Salt Lake has been compared to the Middle East's very salty Dead Sea. The lake has been nicknamed "America's Dead Sea." It is, in fact, the largest saltwater lake in the Western Hemisphere.

Most of the time, the Great Salt Lake is larger than the states of Delaware and Rhode Island combined. Why is it larger only *most of the time*? The reason is that the Great Salt Lake's size is always changing. There is new concern, however, that the Great Salt Lake is threatened by permanent shrinkage, possibly due to human impact.

Four rivers feed into the Great Salt Lake. Depending on how dry the environment is, as well as how much water is flowing into the lake, the size of the Great Salt Lake changes. As an example, in 1873, the lake reached its largest area at 2,400 square miles; but, in 1963, it covered its smallest area at 950 square miles. What has alarmed scientists is that, in July 2021, the Great Salt Lake reached its lowest water level ever. There are two possible causes for the shrinking water level. First, human activity over the past century and a half has diverted water from the feeder rivers for agriculture and other human use. Second, recent droughts and higher-than-normal temperatures have also impacted the amount of water going into the basin.

Although scientists do note that the amount of precipitation within the basin has not changed significantly with the recent changes to the Great Salt Lake, there has been increasing desiccation, or drying out of the lake. This could mean the loss of vital natural habitat for birds. The Great Salt Lake hosts the largest breeding colony of American white pelicans, as well as numerous other birds. Also, further hazards such as dust and other pollutants may become exposed with a shrinking lake, thus creating dangers for both the environment and humans.

10. What is the main idea of this passage?
    A. The Great Salt Lake's thriving ecology is diverse.
    B. The Great Salt Lake is in danger of permanent shrinkage.
    C. The Great Salt Lake changed in size in 1963.
    D. The Great Salt Lake has been affected by humans.

11. How have humans impacted the Great Salt Lake?

    _____

    _____

Algebra/Grammar

DAY 13

Determine the two consecutive integers that each number lies between on a number line.

1. $\sqrt{27}$　　　2. $\sqrt{50}$　　　3. $\sqrt{89}$

Rewrite each list to show the numbers in order from least to greatest.

4. $4, 5, \sqrt{29}, \sqrt{17}$　　　5. $\sqrt{19}, 3, 7, \sqrt{51}$　　　6. $\sqrt{24}, 4, \sqrt{39}, 5$

Verb *tense* shows when an action takes place. If there are two or more verbs in a sentence, their tenses are usually the same. Verb *number* shows whether the verb goes with a singular or a plural subject. Rewrite each sentence to correct each error in verb tense or verb number.

7. After school I will go to orchestra rehearsal, and then I walk home.

8. The top row of books were very dusty.

9. The number of job applicants are much higher than Mr. Pappas expected.

10. When Leo visited Boston, he goes to see the site of the first battle of the Revolutionary War.

CHARACTER CHECK: Express empathy for a friend or family member who needs it.

DAY 13

Writing/Fitness

An *introvert* is defined as an individual who focuses inward, on their own thoughts. An *extrovert* is an individual who focuses more on the external world. Introverts are typically thought of as quiet and maybe shy, while extroverts are often viewed as more outgoing. Would you describe yourself as an introvert or an extrovert or both? Explain your thinking.

_____
_____
_____
_____
_____
_____

Butterfly Kicks

There are many exercises that are perfect for warming up our bodies and getting us moving. Butterfly kicks are one of those exercises. They require nothing more than a flat surface to lie on.

Lie down on your back and stick your legs straight out. Pretend that you are swimming. While keeping your knees straight, lift your legs about a foot from the ground and kick your legs in a fluttering motion. If you have an elastic band, then you can put it around your knees to keep them together. Try to kick your legs for 20 seconds, then lower them several inches and repeat. Is this exercise easier as your legs get closer to the ground? Is it easier when your legs are farther away from the ground?

FITNESS FLASH: Do 10 burpees.

* See page ii.

Algebra/Grammar

DAY 14

Use graphing, substitutions, or elimination to solve these systems of linear equations.

1. $5y - 2x = -1$ and $10y + 2x = 10$

   $x =$ _____ and $y =$ _____

2. $z - w = 25$ and $2z + w = 17$

   $z =$ _____ and $w =$ _____

3. $3a + 4b = 4.5$ and $6a - b = 2.25$

   $a =$ _____ and $b =$ _____

4. $11c - 2d = 100$ and $-5c + 10d = 100$

   $c =$ _____ and $d =$ _____

5. $m - 8n = 10$ and $-m + 16n = 1$

   $m =$ _____ and $n =$ _____

6. $p + r = 10$ and $r - p = 1.4$

   $p =$ _____ and $r =$ _____

A *modifier* is a word or group of words that describes a noun or pronoun. In sentences with a *dangling modifier*, it is unclear what the modifier is describing. Each sentence contains a dangling modifier. Rewrite each sentence to make clear what the modifier is describing.

EXAMPLE: While biking in the park, a bird landed on my handlebars.
While I was biking in the park, a bird landed on my handlebars.

7. Before playing football, the field needed to be cleaned.

   _____

8. After practicing my solo for a week, my music teacher said I would be ready for the concert.

   _____

9. Driving down the dark street, the car's lights were on.

   _____

10. Jumping out of the waves, we saw both dolphins and whales when we went sailing.

    _____

11. Finished with my watercolor painting, my art teacher said I was ready for oil painting next.

    _____

DAY 14

Reading Comprehension

Read the poem. Then, answer the questions.

October by Robert Frost

O hushed October morning mild,   1
Thy leaves have ripened to the fall;
Tomorrow's wind, if it be wild,
Should waste them all.
The crows above the forest call;   5
Tomorrow they may form and go.
O hushed October morning mild,
Begin the hours of this day slow.
Make the day seem to us less brief.
Hearts not averse to being **beguiled**,   10
Beguile us in the way you know.
Release one leaf at break of day;
At noon release another leaf;
One from our trees, one far away.
Retard the sun with gentle mist;   15
Enchant the land with amethyst.
Slow, slow!
For the grapes' sake, if they were all,
Whose leaves already are burnt with frost,
Whose clustered fruit must else be lost—   20
For the grapes' sake along the wall.

12. What does *beguiled* mean in line 10?
    A. enticed
    B. beautiful
    C. refused
    D. gentle

13. What is the overall theme of the poem? Support your answer with evidence from the poem. _____

14. Do you think the poet prefers fall or winter? Why do you think this? _____

FACTOID: Nearly 75% of your brain is made up of water.

Algebra/Parts of Speech

DAY 15

Identify whether each coordinate pair is a solution to the inequality.

1. $y \leq 2x + 3$
   (0, 0) _____
   (−1, 4) _____
   (2, 7) _____

2. $4x - y > 2$
   (0, 0) _____
   (2, 6) _____
   (−1, −9) _____

Graph each inequality. Make sure to use the correct line type (dashed or solid), and shade correctly.

3. $y > -\frac{1}{2}x - 3$

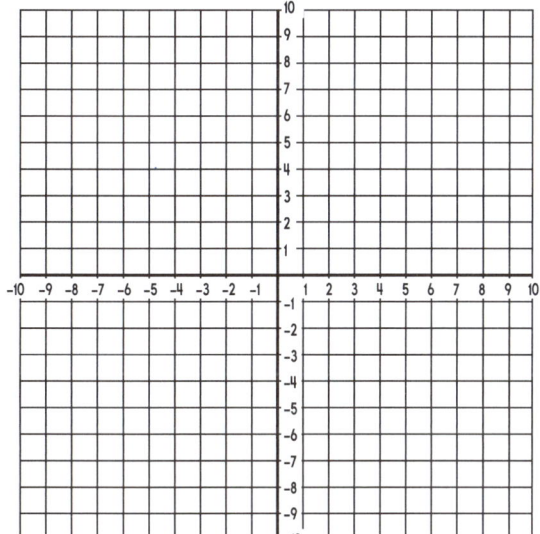

4. $3x + 4y \leq 24$

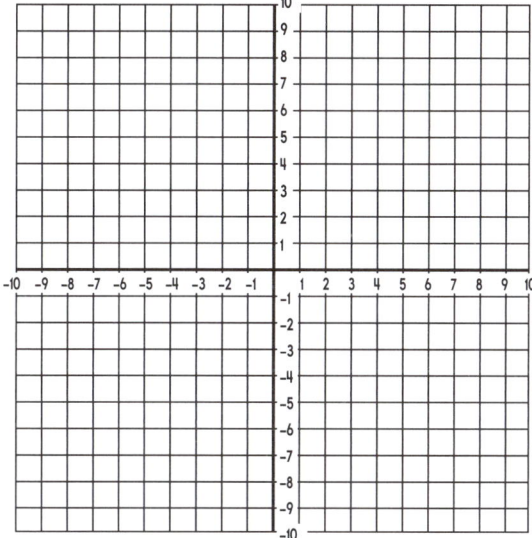

A *participle* is a verb form used as an adjective to modify a noun or pronoun. *Present participles* end in *-ing*. Past participles usually end in *-ed*, but some past participles, like the word *eaten*, are irregular. Underline the participle in each sentence. Then, write the noun or pronoun it modifies on the line.

5. _____ The swimming pool will be closed for cleaning on Sunday.
6. _____ After searching for many years, the art detective finally found the lost painting.
7. _____ Grady made a trail mix with almonds, coconut flakes, and dried apples.
8. _____ Several different fairy tales include a princess and a spinning wheel.
9. _____ I was so happy when the lost puppy was reunited with its owners.

DAY 15

Literary Terms/Science

Just as there are genres of literature, there are different genres of writing. Some of the main types of writing include *expository*, *narrative*, *descriptive*, and *persuasive*. *Expository writing* is informational and is presented in an organized way. *Narrative writing* tells a story; this can be a true experience, a personal narrative, or a fictional story. *Descriptive writing* uses sensory imagery and visuals to describe something. *Persuasive writing* aims to convince the reader to do something or to think something.

Choose a genre of writing that best matches each title. Write the genre on the line.

10. When I Learned to Ride My Bike _____
11. The Life of Walt Disney _____
12. My Experience as a Barista _____
13. The Beauty of Magnolia Trees _____
14. Start Recycling . . . or Else _____
15. The Battle of Bull Run _____

Read the clues that describe each animal. Write the correct word from the word bank for each set of clues.

| anemone | desert tortoise | zebra | wolf |

16. I am a mammal.
    I am in the *Canis* genus.
    I am part of a pack.
    My preferred meal may consist of deer or elk.
    Which animal am I? _____

17. I am a mammal.
    I am in the Equidae class.
    I live on land.
    Other herbivores such as giraffes are my main competition for food.
    Which animal am I? _____

18. I am a carnivore.
    I am in the *Monactis* genus.
    I come in many vibrant colors.
    My symbiotic relationship with clownfish is well known.
    Which animal am I? _____

19. I live on land.
    I am in the *Gopherus* genus.
    I am an herbivore.
    My egg clutches are usually laid between May and July.
    Which animal am I? _____

CHARACTER CHECK: Complete a random act of kindness for someone today.

Geometry/Vocabulary

DAY 16

In each dilation below, Point A stays the same, while Point B moves to new coordinates. Find the new coordinates of each Point B.

1. Point A of a circle is located at (2, 2). Point B is located on the opposite edge of the circle at (4, 2). If the circle is dilated by a scale factor of 4, then what are the new coordinates of Point B?

   _____

2. Point A is the top-left vertex of a square, and it is located at (1, 4). Point B is the top-right vertex of the square, and it is located at (5, 4). If the square is dilated by a scale factor of 3, then what are the new coordinates of Point B?

   _____

3. Point A is a vertex of the base of a triangle, and it is located at (3, 3). Point B is the opposite vertex of the base of the triangle, and it is located at (6, 3). If the circle is dilated by a scale factor of 2, then what are the new coordinates of Point B?

   _____

Use context clues in each sentence to help determine the meaning of the underlined word. Write what the underlined word means. Circle the words in the sentence that helped you determine the meaning.

4. I strongly abhor bananas; I will do anything to avoid that taste.
   _____

5. I left an anonymous note in the suggestion box, as I forgot to include my name.
   _____

6. The ball ricocheted off the wall and nearly hit me in the head.
   _____

7. The old house was filled with cobwebs and dust, and it seemed uninhabitable.
   _____

8. The evidence was irrefutable, as the defense attorney could not disprove its accuracy.
   _____

9. The toddler remained obstinate and refused to put on shoes.
   _____

DAY 16

Reading Comprehension/Social Studies

Read the passage. Then, answer the questions.

The Legacy of the Lobster

When European settlers began living in New England, lobsters were very plentiful and could easily be harvested, as they just washed ashore. But people grew weary of eating them, so lobsters were used to feed prisoners. Over time, the **abundance** of lobsters along the East Coast began to dwindle, and the shellfish began to be seen as a delicacy, appreciated by people across the country. The price of lobster began to rise. Today, lobster is sold at market price, meaning that the cost varies based on daily supply.

10. What is the meaning of the word *abundance* as it is used in the passage?
    - A. scarcity
    - B. high demand
    - C. large supply
    - D. uniqueness

11. Are there more or fewer lobsters today than there were 300 years ago? Explain how you know. _____

12. Have you ever eaten lobster? If so, then what did you like or dislike about it? If not, do you think you would like or dislike it? Why? _____

Write the letter of each type of government next to the phrase that describes it.

| A. monarchy | B. democracy | C. republic | D. aristocracy |
| E. oligarchy | F. theocracy | G. autocracy | H. plutocracy |

13. _____ a form of government in which the wealthy rule
14. _____ a form of government in which nobility rules
15. _____ a form of government in which the people rule
16. _____ a form of government in which one person rules through inheritance, such as a queen or king
17. _____ a form of government in which religious leaders rule
18. _____ a form of government in which leaders are elected
19. _____ a form of government in which a small group rules
20. _____ a form of government in which one person, such as a dictator, rules but not necessarily by inheriting the position

Geometry/Parts of Speech

DAY 17

Describe a sequence of transformations from triangle ABC to triangle A'B'C' that proves they are similar.

1.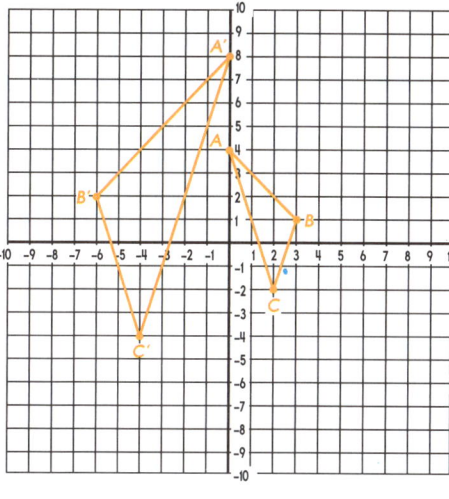

2.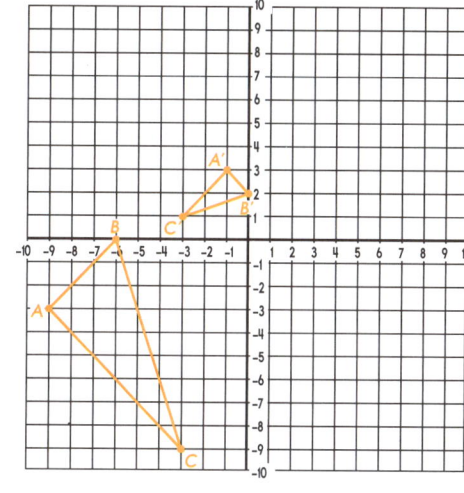

_____   _____

_____   _____

A *predicate nominative* is a noun or pronoun that follows a linking verb and renames or describes the sentence's subject. Read each sentence. Circle the predicate nominative, and underline the linking verb. Then, draw an arrow from the predicate nominative to the subject it renames.

3. Tokyo and Delhi are the two most populous cities in the world.
4. Qin Shi Huang was the first emperor of China.
5. The deepest point on Earth is the Mariana Trench in the Pacific Ocean.
6. The Alps are mountains that stretch across much of the European continent.
7. Queen Elizabeth II has been the queen of England since 1952.
8. Washington, D.C., became the capital of the United States on July 16, 1790.

 **FITNESS FLASH:** Do 15 side crunches to the left and 15 side crunches to the right.

* See page ii.

DAY 17

Reading Comprehension

Read the passage. Then, answer the questions.

Did Betsy Ross Really Create the First American Flag?

The woman who is popularly credited with the creation of the American flag is Betsy Ross. There is evidence that suggests, however, that she may not have actually made it.

Ross was born in Philadelphia on January 1, 1752, as Elizabeth Griscom. After attending a Quaker school, she apprenticed as an upholsterer. When she was 21, in 1773, she eloped with John Ross, a non-Quaker, in New Jersey. Together, they set up an upholstery business. Sadly, John Ross died less than two years into the marriage.

As a widow, Ross continued running her seamstress business. Popular accounts state that George Washington, then commander of the Continental Army fighting in the Revolutionary War, visited Ross in 1776 or 1777 concerning a design for a flag for the new country. Ross then presented Washington with the first design of the stars and stripes version of the American flag.

Betsy Ross certainly sewed flags during these years. She created a flag for the Pennsylvania Navy. She also provided tents for the Continental Army. Historians have found no **credible** evidence, however, that she really created the first American flag. When Betsy Ross died in 1836, she had no idea that she would be incorrectly credited for creating a major American symbol.

So why was she given credit for it? The issue first started in 1870 when Ross's grandson, while giving a speech to the Historical Society of Pennsylvania, credited her with sewing the flag for Washington and a congressional committee. This likely false story quickly spread, being picked up by highly popular magazines. It was soon taken as fact.

So, who really created the first flag? Evidence points to Francis Hopkinson, a signer of the Declaration of Independence from New Jersey. In 1780, he sent a bill to the Continental Congress for designing the flag, as well as for the country's Great Seal.

9. According to the passage, how did the legend of the Betsy Ross flag start?
   - A. through a speech
   - B. through a publication
   - C. through a war
   - D. through Congress

10. What is the meaning of the word *credible* as it is used in this passage?
    - A. amazing
    - B. hypothetical
    - C. reliable
    - D. untrue

11. How is the claim that Francis Hopkinson designed the first flag supported by evidence?

_____

_____

Functions/Parts of Speech

DAY 18

Use the relationship shown in each table to write a linear equation in slope-intercept form.

1.

x	y
0	−3
1	3
2	6

y = _____

2.

x	y
0	6
−1	$5\frac{1}{5}$
−2	$4\frac{2}{5}$

y = _____

3.

x	y
2	−5
4	−7
6	−9

y = _____

4.

x	y
−1	$-\frac{5}{8}$
−2	$-\frac{7}{4}$
−3	$-\frac{23}{8}$

y = _____

5.

x	y
−2	−1
2	3
4	5

y = _____

6.

x	y
$\frac{1}{2}$	$-\frac{5}{6}$
$\frac{3}{2}$	−1
$\frac{5}{2}$	$-\frac{7}{6}$

y = _____

Verb tense shows when an action takes place. Write the past tense and future tense of each present tense verb. Then, use a dictionary to check your work.

	Present	Past	Future
7.	bring	_____	_____
8.	sing	_____	_____
9.	seek	_____	_____
10.	tear	_____	_____
11.	sneeze	_____	_____
12.	swim	_____	_____
13.	catch	_____	_____
14.	begin	_____	_____
15.	buy	_____	_____
16.	teach	_____	_____

DAY 18

Literary Terms/Science

Are you ever warned to "watch your tone"? Words and writing have a *tone*, which is the attitude of the writer or speaker. Tones can be formal or informal. Any writing for school or work should be written in a formal tone, while narratives or more casual messages or emails can often be written in an informal tone.

Read each of the sentences and decide if there is a *formal* or *informal* tone used.

17. _____ The carnival hosts 20 rides, 10 arcade stations, and 4 food vendors.
18. _____ We did an experiment in class today.
19. _____ The results of the investigation were conclusive that the powder was acidic.
20. _____ An officer is investigating the scene for any evidence.
21. _____ Do you feel okay or not?
22. _____ For how many more miles will we be hiking on this trail?

Sir Isaac Newton is one of the most famous physicists of all time. He is well known for his scientific laws of motion. These laws describe force, inertia, motion, and reactions. If you are not familiar with these laws, look them up online. Read the clues that describe each of Newton's laws. Write the correct number of the law (1, 2, or 3) that matches each clue. Each law will be used more than once.

23. _____ The force applied to a large box by a person can be calculated if we know the mass of the box and how fast it is accelerating.
24. _____ A ball is rolled, and the only reason it stops is because friction acts upon it to slow it down.
25. _____ If a billiard cue hits a billiard ball, then the cue will stop moving, and the billiard ball will start moving.
26. _____ When a baseball player catches a ball, the ball exerts a certain amount of force on the glove, and the glove exerts the same amount of force back on the ball.
27. _____ The mass of a bowling ball can be determined if we know how fast it accelerates down a bowling alley lane and how much force it exerts on the bowling pins.
28. _____ Trees do not move unless wind blows on them and forces them to sway.

CHARACTER CHECK: Write about something embarrassing that has happened to you. What did you learn from the event?

Geometry/Data Analysis

DAY 19

Two figures are *similar* if one can be obtained from the other using a sequence of rotations, reflections, translations, or dilations. Show that each pair of figures is similar by describing one or more transformations that can be used to obtain the second figure from the first.

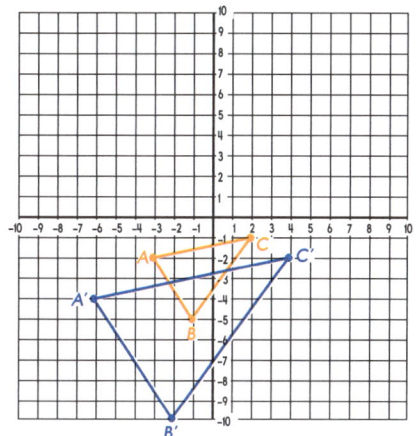 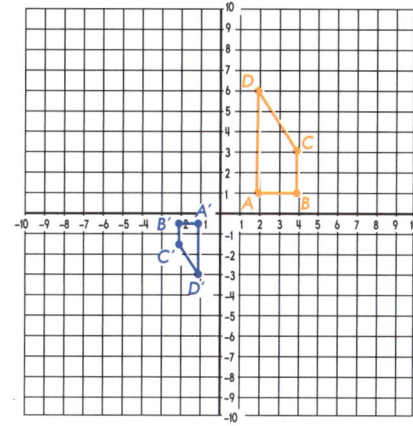 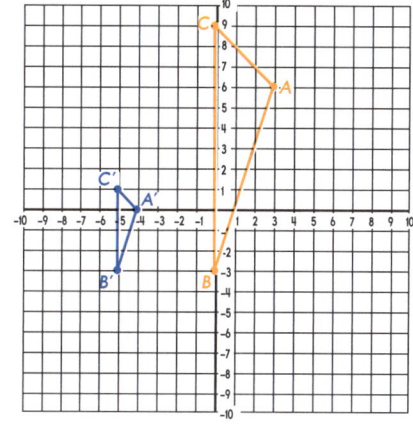

1. Sequence of transformations: _____

2. Sequence of transformations: _____

3. Sequence of transformations: _____

The *mean* of a data set is found by finding the sum of all values and dividing by the number of values in the set. Calculate the mean of the given data sets.

4. 11, 15, 7, 13, 14

    _____

5. 8, 13, 7, 16, 19, 3

    _____

6. Students in Mr. Smith's math class earned the following grades on a test:
    65, 72, 81, 93, 48, 100, 96, 56, 67, 74, 87, 91
    What was the mean score on the test?

    _____

7. The mean on Ms. Hasan's test was a score of 82%. The scores were as follows:
    76, 82, 93, 98, 85, 68, 92, 86, x
    What is the value of the missing score, x?

    _____

DAY 19

Language Arts/Writing

Personification is when a nonhuman object is given human qualities. For example, in the sentence "The angry blister was covered with a bandage," a blister is not a living thing and would not have human traits such as anger.

Underline the examples of personification in each sentence.

8. The wind howled fiercely during the night.
9. The plant thirstily drank the water.
10. The leaves danced across the street as the wind gently pushed them.
11. The aroma of the freshly baked cookies whispered my name.
12. Time refused to move as the end of the day approached.
13. The truck was tired and thirsty as it pulled into the rest area.
14. The sun peeked out shyly from behind the clouds.
15. The garbage disposal roared its appreciation for its meal of food scraps.

People often describe themselves as either being a *morning person* (someone who likes to get up and get going early in the day) or perhaps a *night owl* (someone who likes to stay up late). Do you consider yourself a night owl, a morning person, or neither one? Explain why and provide examples of what makes you fit into that category or why you do not fit into either.

_____
_____
_____
_____
_____
_____

 **FITNESS FLASH:** Do 3 sets of butterfly kicks for 20 seconds.

* See page ii.

Algebra/Parts of Speech

DAY 20

Add or subtract to solve the expressions.

1. $(3x + 2) + (2x) =$ _____
2. $(3a + 5) - (6a - 2) =$ _____
3. $9r + 7 - 2r + 1 =$ _____
4. $2b - 3 + 7b - 4 =$ _____
5. $(5z + 4) + (z + 6) + 2z =$ _____
6. $(4c - 1) - (6c - 3) =$ _____
7. $(17z - 4) + (2z + 6) + 7z =$ _____
8. $(14c - 11) + (2c - 8) =$ _____

There are many parts of speech: verbs, nouns, adjectives, adverbs, prepositions, etc. Name the part of speech of the underlined word in each sentence.

9. Mt. Kilimanjaro, which is in Africa, is the world's <u>tallest</u> freestanding mountain.
   _____

10. Mt. Kilimanjaro is very tall; <u>however</u>, it is not the world's tallest mountain.
    _____

11. Mt. Everest, in Asia, is the tallest mountain, with its <u>peak</u> at 8,848 meters.
    _____

12. Mt. Everest, like many other mountains, is part of a <u>range</u>.
    _____

13. Mt. Kilimanjaro was formed by a <u>volcanic</u> eruption.
    _____

14. Mt. Kilimanjaro is <u>located</u> on the equator.
    _____

Write your own sentence. Underline the noun, circle the verb, and put a box around the adjective.

_____

FACTOID: Caterpillars have two sets of six eyes!

DAY 20

Reading Comprehension

Read the passage. Then, answer the questions.

The Incredible Shrinking Computer

As defined by Merriam-Webster Dictionary, a computer is "an electronic machine that can store and work with large amounts of information." The first computer that fits this definition was the Z1, built in 1936 by Konrad Zuse of Germany. It filled his parents' living room, but was only able to compute four arithmetic functions.

Computers have become more complex, yet smaller, since the Z1. Americans John Mauchly and John P. Eckert invented the Electronic Numerical Integrator and Computer in 1946. This machine, better known as ENIAC, was the first general computer, and sat in a 50-by-30-foot space.

Large computers like ENIAC were used throughout the 1950s mostly by engineers and scientists. This changed in 1965 when the Programma 101 was introduced as one of the first types of desktop calculator. This Italian invention was widely adopted and copied. The development of computers was happening so quickly that American businessperson and engineer Gordon Moore theorized in 1965 that computers would steadily become more powerful and smaller. This theory was nicknamed "Moore's Law." The developments of the 1960s paved the way for the creation in the 1970s of more versatile computers that could be used by individuals. These "personal computers," or PCs, could be used by people in their homes. Technological advances were furthered by the introduction of Apple's Macintosh in 1984.

Computers through the 1990s steadily became more powerful, but the introduction of Apple's iPhone changed everything. These handheld devices had more computing power than earlier, larger computers, and they could be carried around in one's pocket. This type of technology, including touch screens and the later invention of tablets, has made computing technology so commonplace that, as of 2021, 97% of Americans own a mobile device—that is, they own a computer.

15. How were early computers different from modern computers?
    A. Early computers were smaller and less complex.
    B. Early computers were larger and more complex.
    C. Early computers were smaller and more complex.
    D. Early computers were larger and less complex.

16. How does "Moore's Law" seem to be correct?
    _____

17. What changes do you think might be made to computers of the future, based on what you read in the passage?
    _____
    _____

Science Experiment

BONUS

Are You a Supertaster?

How many taste buds do you have?

Different areas of your tongue are responsible for sensing each of the five different food tastes: salty, sour, bitter, sweet, and umami. Everyone senses each of these tastes at different intensities. Some people are considered supertasters. These supertasters may have more taste buds than the average person and are able to taste certain tastes more intensely. Supertasters tend to be picky eaters because flavors may be too strong for them, especially bitter flavors like those found in spinach or other vegetables.
In this experiment, you will count the number of taste buds you have to see if you could be a supertaster too! Then, you will compare your taste-bud count to those of the people in your family.

Materials:
- wax paper
- hole punch
- blue food coloring
- flashlight
- scissors
- water

Procedure:
1. Cut a small square about one-half inch long from the wax paper. Punch a hole in your wax paper square.

2. Drop a small amount of blue food coloring on your tongue. Have a sip of water and swish it around in your mouth. Spit the water out. Most of your tongue will have turned blue, with the exception of small, pink circles called fungiform papillae (taste buds).

3. Place your wax paper square on your tongue.

4. Using the flashlight, count each pink circle (fungiform papillae) within the circle of the wax paper.

5. Record the number of fungiform papillae you have under the wax paper here: _____. If you have more than 30 fungiform papillae, you are a supertaster!

6. Ask your family members to complete the same task. Compare their results to yours and discuss foods that you all like and dislike.
Do you find that certain foods are too bitter for you to enjoy? If so, which ones?

_____

Do you see a pattern in the number of fungiform papillae on your tongue and the types of food you enjoy? Do you see a pattern in the results for other members of your family and the types of foods they like or dislike?

_____

_____

BONUS

Science Experiment

Testing pH

Is it an acid or a base?

All solutions have a pH level, which tells us how acidic or basic something is. In this experiment, you will use cabbage juice as a pH indicator, noting if substances are acidic or basic based on how the solution changes color.

Materials:
- clear plastic or glass cups
- red cabbage
- boiling water
- strainer
- household solutions for testing (vinegar, citrus juices, milk, baking soda, laundry detergent, etc.)

Procedure:

First, create your cabbage juice (with adult supervision). Chop up some red cabbage and either pour boiling water onto it or add it to a blender with boiling water and then puree. Wait 10 minutes so the color can leach out of the cabbage, then use a strainer or filter to remove the solids. Distribute the liquid into several different cups for testing. **Make sure to never combine different solutions. Use a new cup of cabbage juice for each solution you test.**

Into separate cups of cabbage juice, one at a time, add water to one, vinegar or a citrus juice to another, hand soap or laundry detergent to another, and any other household substances you want to test to other cups. As you add each substance, note any change in color on the lines below.

_____

_____

Using the table below, determine the pH of each substance you tested. Write your results below.

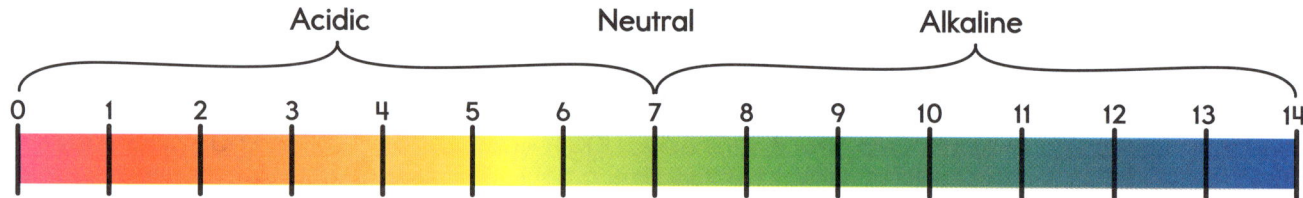

Results

Substance	pH
water	7

Of the solutions that you tested, which substance is the most acidic? Which one is the most basic? How do you know?

_____

_____

_____

_____

Social Studies Activity

BONUS

European Explorers

Use textbooks, the internet, and reference guides to help you identify these explorers.

1. Portuguese explorer who in 1498 was the first European to reach India by sailing around the continent of Africa

   _____

2. French explorer who made three voyages to North America and in the 1530s and 1540s explored the St. Lawrence River, claiming sections of North America for France

   _____

3. Italian navigator who in 1492 sailed for Spain to seek a shorter route to Asia but found the Americas instead

   _____

4. Italian explorer who sailed for England and made voyages to North America in the 1490s, laying claim to parts of Canada for that country

   _____

5. Spanish explorer whose 1519–1522 expedition was the first to circumnavigate the world; he did not survive the voyage

   _____

6. Spanish conquistador who traveled and explored the southeastern part of the United States in the late 1530s and early 1540s; he and his expedition companions were the first Europeans to see the Mississippi River

   _____

7. English explorer who sailed for both England and the Netherlands in the early 1600s, laying claim to what is now New York for the Dutch

   _____

8. Italian explorer who is best known for creating a map that placed his name on two continents; the map is still used today

   _____

9. Spanish conquistador who explored Florida in 1513 looking for an island named Bimini, which reportedly had a "fountain of youth"

   _____

10. Spanish conquistador who explored Central America and was the first European to see the Pacific Ocean from the Americas

    _____

BONUS

Social Studies Activity

Translating the Bill of Rights (continued)

The first ten amendments to the U.S. Constitution are called the Bill of Rights. These amendments provide important protections to American citizens and help to support a democratic society. Sometimes these amendments are hard to understand, however, because of the way they were written centuries ago. In this activity, read the amendments of the Bill of Rights. Then, in the space provided, summarize the meaning of the amendment in plain language.

1. **Fifth Amendment**
   No person shall be held to answer for a capital, or otherwise infamous crime, unless on a presentment or indictment of a Grand Jury, except in cases arising in the land or naval forces, or in the Militia, when in actual service in time of War or public danger; nor shall any person be subject for the same offence to be twice put in jeopardy of life or limb; nor shall be compelled in any criminal case to be a witness against himself, nor be deprived of life, liberty, or property, without due process of law; nor shall private property be taken for public use, without just compensation.

   _____
   _____
   _____

2. **Sixth Amendment**
   In all criminal prosecutions, the accused shall enjoy the right to a speedy and public trial, by an impartial jury of the State and district wherein the crime shall have been committed, which district shall have been previously ascertained by law, and to be informed of the nature and cause of the accusation; to be confronted with the witnesses against him; to have compulsory process for obtaining witnesses in his favor, and to have the Assistance of Counsel for his defence.

   _____
   _____
   _____

3. **Seventh Amendment**
   In Suits at common law, where the value in controversy shall exceed twenty dollars, the right of trial by jury shall be preserved, and no fact tried by a jury, shall be otherwise re-examined in any Court of the United States, than according to the rules of the common law.

   _____
   _____
   _____

Timeline of the Civil Rights Movement

There were many important events that led to breakthroughs in civil rights for African Americans in the 20th century. Read the descriptions of the individual events. Then, do research to find the years they occurred. Write the number of each event in the correct place on the timeline.

1. Dr. Martin Luther King, Jr. gives his "I Have a Dream" speech, and 250,000 people participate in the "March on Washington" to demand equality.

2. In *Brown v. Board of Education*, the Supreme Court rules that segregation in schools is unconstitutional.

3. African American and white activists ride buses through the South in protest to segregated bussing in what became known as the "Freedom Rides."

4. President Lyndon B. Johnson signs into law the Voting Rights Act, which prohibits states from requiring a literacy test for the right to vote.

5. Rosa Parks refuses to give up her seat to a white man on a bus, setting off the Montgomery bus boycott.

6. President Harry Truman ends segregation in the military with Executive Order 9981.

7. Martin Luther King Jr. is assassinated; and the Fair Housing Act, which provides equal opportunities in housing, is signed into law.

8. Nine African American students are blocked from integrating into a white high school in Little Rock, Arkansas.

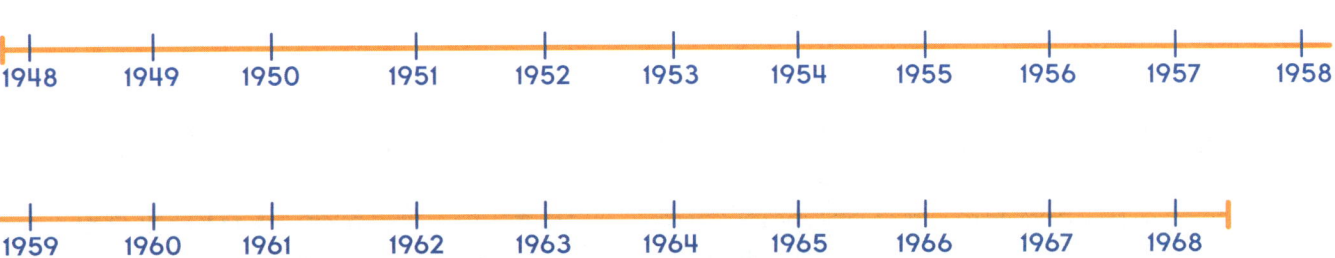

BONUS

Outdoor Extension Activities

Take It Outside!

On a cloudy day, set up a blanket outside and watch the clouds go by. Tell what each cloud looks like to you. In a notebook, sketch a picture of one of your favorite clouds that you see. Do you know what types of clouds these are?

Go for a walk around your neighborhood or at a nearby park. While on your walk, look for examples of geometry. Try to find examples of each of the following:

- sphere
- cube
- rectangular prism
- cylinder
- cone
- parallel lines
- perpendicular lines
- right angles
- obtuse angles
- acute angles
- straight angles

Which of these things was easiest to find? Which was most difficult?

In an outdoor space, design an obstacle course. Your obstacle course should include elements that require the following:

- something to climb
- running for some distance
- hopping for some distance
- something to go under
- something to go over

Find a friend to complete your obstacle course. Encourage your friend to develop a similar course for you to complete, or time yourselves to see who can complete the course in a shorter time period.

* See page ii.

SECTION III

Monthly Goals

Think of three goals to set for yourself this month. For example, you may want to learn five new vocabulary words each week. Write your goals on the lines. Post them somewhere that you will see them every day.

Draw a check mark beside each goal you meet. Feel proud that you have met your goals and continue to set new ones to challenge yourself.

1. _____
2. _____
3. _____

Word List

The following words are used in this section. Use a dictionary to look up each word that you do not know. Then, write three sentences. Use at least one word from the word list in each sentence.

abbreviated	pilfer
formidable	porous
illegible	reprieve
luminous	smite
malicious	

1. _____
_____
2. _____
_____
3. _____
_____

SECTION III

Introduction to Endurance

This section includes fitness and character development activities that focus on endurance. These activities are designed to get you moving and thinking about developing your physical and mental stamina. If you have limited mobility, feel free to modify any suggested exercises to fit your individual abilities.

Physical Endurance

What do climbing stairs, jogging, and riding your bike have in common? They are all great ways to build endurance! Having endurance means performing an activity for a period of time before your body becomes tired. Improving your endurance requires regular aerobic exercise, which causes your heart to beat faster. You also breathe harder. As a result of regular aerobic activity, your heart becomes stronger, and your blood cells deliver oxygen to your body more efficiently.

Although there are times when a relaxing activity is valuable, it is important to take advantage of the warm mornings and sunny days to go outside. Choose activities that you enjoy. Invite a family member to go for a walk or a bike ride. Play a game of basketball with friends. Leave the relaxing activities for when it is dark, too hot, or raining.

Set an endurance goal this summer. For example, you might jog every day until you can run one mile without stopping. Set new goals when you meet your old ones. Be proud of your endurance success!

Mental Endurance

Showing mental endurance means persevering. Continuing with tasks when you might want to quit and working until they are done are ways that you can show mental endurance.

Build your mental endurance this summer. Maybe you want to earn some extra money for a new bike by helping your neighbors with yard work. But, after one week of working in your neighbors' yards, it is not as easy as you thought it would be. Think about some key points, such as how you have wanted that new bike for months. Be positive. Remind yourself that you have been working for only one week and that your neighbors are very appreciative of your work. Think of ways to make the yard work more enjoyable, such as starting earlier in the day or listening to music while you work. Quitting should be the last resort. Build your mental endurance now. It will help prepare you for challenges later.

Geometry/Language Arts

DAY 1

A right triangle with legs *a* and *b* will have hypotenuse *c*. Use the Pythagorean theorem, $a^2 + b^2 = c^2$, to determine the missing dimension in each right triangle. Round answers to the nearest tenth as needed.

1. a = 8 in.
   b = 15 in.
   c = _____ in.

2. a = 63 cm
   b = _____ cm
   c = 65 cm

3. a = _____ ft.
   b = 2.3 ft.
   c = 26.5 ft.

4. a = 7 yd.
   b = 3 yd.
   c = _____ yd.

5. a = 5 m
   b = _____ m
   c = 8 m

6. a = 10.8 ft.
   b = 11.4 ft.
   c = _____ ft.

Many nonfiction books contain features that convey or organize information in different ways for the reader. Write the letter of the correct book feature next to its definition.

| A. bibliography | B. table of contents | C. title page | D. index | E. caption |
| F. glossary | G. heading | H. pictures | I. boldfaced words | J. diagram |

7. _____ an alphabetical list of important vocabulary words and their definitions

8. _____ a list of reference books, articles, and websites you can use to find more information about the subject you are reading about, usually in the back of the book

9. _____ an alphabetical list at the back of the book that includes people, places, key words, or topics in the text, with page numbers for quick reference

10. _____ a description or explanation for a photograph or illustration

11. _____ a page at the front of the book listing the book title and author, and usually the publisher

12. _____ a list of chapters and page numbers at the beginning of the book

13. _____ photographs or illustrations

14. _____ words or phrases written in darker print to emphasize importance and to show which words are in the glossary

15. _____ a detailed picture of an object from the text, with labels that name or explain the important parts

16. _____ a short line of text that usually identifies the main idea for that section of text

DAY 1

Vocabulary/Algebra

Use context clues to write the correct word from the word bank to complete each sentence.

| feudal | contours | brazen | intangible | flank |

17. The journalist was asked to leave the press conference after making some _____ remarks to the police chief.

18. Before the actor went on stage, the stylist applied makeup to the _____ of his face to highlight his cheekbones.

19. Large flags _____ the front door of the office building.

20. During medieval times, many societies had _____ systems in which land was given out in exchange for military service.

21. Instead of giving us traditional birthday gifts each year, my grandfather gives us something _____, like taking us to a baseball game.

Simplify each expression. Write your answers in standard form.

22. $(4 \times 10^{-5}) + (2 \times 10^{-6}) =$ _____

23. $(5.2 \times 10^4) \times 3 =$ _____

24. $(1 \times 10^7) \div 4 =$ _____

25. $(6.43 \times 10^{-2}) \times (1 \times 10^3) =$ _____

26. $(2.4 \times 10^6) + (7.8 \times 10^8) =$ _____

27. $(3.45 \times 10^7) - (5.02 \times 10^6) =$ _____

28. $(1.35 \times 10^2) - (2.07 \times 10^3) =$ _____

FACTOID: Strawberries have their seeds on the outside, and they are the only fruit like this.

Geometry/Algebra

DAY 2

Use the Pythagorean theorem to find the missing side lengths in each figure. Round answers to the nearest tenth if necessary.

1.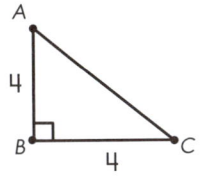

   AC = _____

2.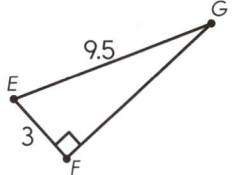

   FG = _____

3.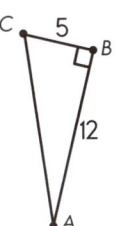

   AC = _____

4.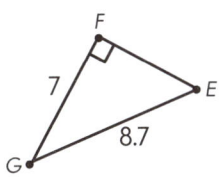

   FE = _____

5.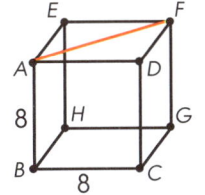

   AF = _____

6.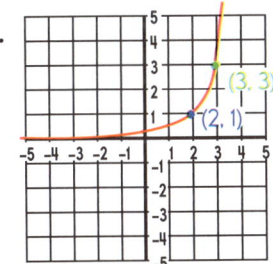

   BG = _____

   AG = _____

Match the exponential function to its graph by verifying that the points on the graph are solutions to the equation. Circle the letter of the correct graph.

7. $y = 3^x - 2$

   A.
   B.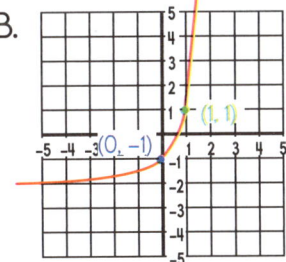
   C.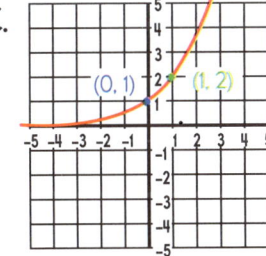

Match the graph to its function rule by verifying that the points on the graph are solutions to the equation. Circle the letter of the correct function rule below.

8.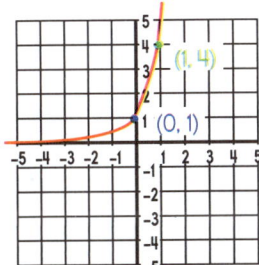

   A. $y = 2^x$
   B. $y = 2^x + 1$
   C. $y = 4^x$
   D. $y = 4x + 1$

DAY 2

Vocabulary/Writing

Choose the correct word from the word bank to complete each sentence. Use context clues to help you choose the words.

| smite | malicious | luminous | formidable | pilfer |

9. The squirrels will often _____ birdseed from the bird feeder and store it in the tree.

10. Because the player's actions on the soccer field were _____, the referee told that player to leave the game.

11. The villain in the movie promised to _____ anyone who mistreated him.

12. After we lost power, the _____ candle provided enough light for us to play a game of cards before bed.

13. The talented and _____ chess champion inspired her opponents to become better players.

How do you think life as a teenager is different from life as a young child? What things are easier for you now that you are a teenager? What things are more difficult? Use another piece of paper if you need more space.

_____
_____
_____
_____
_____
_____
_____
_____

FITNESS FLASH: Use a wall to do a wall sit for 20 seconds.

*See page ii.

Multiplication/Parts of Speech

DAY 3

Without the use of a calculator, find the product of the following pairs of integers.

1. 34 × 52 _____
2. 471 × 13 _____
3. 50 × 103 _____
4. 143 × 519 _____
5. 534 × 100 _____
6. 122 × 417 _____
7. 20 × 109 _____
8. 125 × 25 _____

A *gerund* is a verb that is used as a noun. A gerund is formed by adding *-ing* to a base verb. Circle the gerund in each sentence. Then, write its base verb on the line.

9. _____ My grandmother and I enjoy cooking some of our favorite family recipes together.
10. _____ Washing hands is an important way to stay healthy during cold and flu season.
11. _____ I would recommend arriving at the airport at least two hours before your flight leaves.
12. _____ While I read my book on the couch, I also love sipping a cup of tea.
13. _____ Eating breakfast for dinner is something fun that my family likes to do every once in a while.
14. _____ Emily and Hanna like walking to school together in the spring when the weather is nice.
15. _____ Surfing is a sport that I have always wanted to try.

DAY 3

Reading Comprehension

Read the recipe. Then, answer the questions.

Delicious Peach Cobbler

Ingredients

- $\frac{1}{2}$ cup unsalted butter
- 1 cup all-purpose flour
- 2 cups sugar, divided
- 1 tablespoon baking powder
- pinch of salt
- 1 cup milk
- 4 cups fresh or frozen peach slices
- 1 tablespoon lemon juice
- ground cinnamon or nutmeg (optional)

Directions

A. Melt butter in a 13-by 9-inch baking dish.

B. Combine flour, 1 cup sugar, baking powder, and salt; add milk, stirring just until dry ingredients are **moistened**. Pour batter over melted butter (do not stir).

C. Combine remaining 1 cup sugar, peach slices, and lemon juice in a pot and bring to a boil over high heat, stirring constantly; pour over batter (do not stir). Sprinkle with cinnamon, if desired.

D. Bake at 375° for 40 to 45 minutes or until golden brown. Serve the cobbler warm or cool.

16. What ingredients make up the batter in this recipe?
    A. butter, sugar, and milk
    B. sugar, peach slices, and lemon juice
    C. cinnamon, nutmeg, salt, flour, and lemon juice
    D. flour, sugar, baking powder, salt, and milk

17. Which ingredient in this recipe is optional?
    A. milk
    B. lemon juice
    C. cinnamon
    D. baking powder

18. What does *moistened* mean?
    A. slightly wet
    B. soaked
    C. absorbed fully
    D. combined

19. What should you do after you combine the flour, sugar, baking powder, and salt?
    A. Pour batter over butter.
    B. Add milk.
    C. Bring sugar, peaches, and lemon juice to a boil.
    D. Bake for 40 to 45 minutes.

20. Why does the ingredients list say the 2 cups of sugar should be divided?

*Recipe slightly modified from www.southernliving.com/recipes/fresh-peach-cobbler.

Algebra/Language Arts

DAY 4

Solve each system of equations. Write your answer as an ordered pair (x, y).

1. $y = 4x$
   $3x + 7y = -62$
   _____

2. $y = 2x + 5$
   $y = -10x + 53$
   _____

3. $x = -7$
   $4x + 6y = 2$
   _____

4. $-x = y$
   $y = 7x - 24$
   _____

5. $5x - 4y = 46$
   $2x - 8y = 12$
   _____

6. $9x + 3y = 22$
   $x + 2y = 3$
   _____

An *author's* purpose is a reason for writing. Authors typically write to inform, persuade, or entertain. An author who writes to *inform* gives information about a topic. An author who writes to *persuade* tries to convince readers of something. An author who writes to *entertain* writes something that readers will enjoy. Read each passage and answer the question that follows.

7. More than 20,000 honeybees may live together in a single hive. Each hive has a single queen bee and hundreds of drone bees. The remaining members of the colony are the worker bees.
   What is the author's purpose for writing this passage?
   _____

8. Ronan gathered up his belongings, stuffing everything in his backpack as fast as he possibly could. The room fell silent, and all eyes were on him as he rushed out of the classroom. As the door slammed behind him, he felt an enormous sense of relief.
   What is the author's purpose for writing this passage?
   _____

9. Having a dog offers many benefits to families. Welcoming a furry friend into your family can teach younger family members many important values, such as responsibility and compassion. Also, having a dog will likely increase your family's daily dose of physical activity.
   What is the author's purpose for writing this passage?
   _____

DAY 4

Vocabulary/Fitness

Read each sentence. Use context clues to match each boldfaced word with its definition.

A. a rest or break
B. not damaged
C. to look at things in a casual way
D. shortened
E. to occur at the same time
F. to keep something away
G. not clear enough to be read
H. to avoid or neglect a duty
I. to be enough
J. an enemy or opponent

10. _____ We read an **abbreviated** version of Shakespeare's Macbeth instead of the full-length play.
11. _____ Kayla loves to **browse** the new-arrivals section of her favorite bookstore.
12. _____ Planting lavender in your yard may help to **repel** mosquitoes.
13. _____ Vin needed a **reprieve** from doing his homework, so he went for a walk outside.
14. _____ Will decided not to **shirk** his responsibilities at the animal shelter because he knew they needed his help.
15. _____ The date on the back of the old photograph was **illegible**, so I asked my grandmother when it was taken.
16. _____ Alicia's birthday **coincides** with Thanksgiving this year, so it will be an extra-special holiday.
17. _____ Do you need my original birth certificate, or will a copy **suffice**?
18. _____ Matt was ready to face his **adversary** in the final match of the chess tournament.
19. _____ The restaurant remained **intact** despite the flooding caused by the storm.

Walking

Getting daily exercise is an important part of staying healthy. There are so many forms of exercise to choose from: swimming, running, and playing sports. The important thing is to keep moving. Walking can be a good way to get exercise too. Walking is nice because it allows you to move at a relaxed pace and can be done by individuals of all ages.

Going for a walk with a friend or family member is the perfect time to talk about anything that is on your mind, which helps you de-stress and strengthen your relationships. Walking also allows you to connect with nature and can be done just about anywhere. There are many devices, some built into smartphones, that can be used to track the number of steps you take each day, whether you are walking or running. This is a great way to track your fitness goals, and it helps to hold you accountable for getting daily exercise.

Algebra/Parts of Speech

DAY 5

Solve each problem using a system of equations.

1. Arthur is 7 years older than his brother. In 8 years, Arthur will be twice his brother's current age. How old is Arthur now?

   _____

2. There are a total of 33 blue shirts and yellow shirts on a store's shelf. The number of blue shirts is 9 less than twice the number of yellow shirts. How many yellow shirts are on the shelf?

   _____

3. When 3 adults and 5 children visit the city's swimming pool, it costs $13.50. When 5 adults and 6 children visit the pool, it costs $19.00. How much does it cost for 1 adult to visit the pool?

   _____

4. The weight of 7 large packages and 2 small packages is 38 pounds. The weight of 3 large packages and 4 small packages is 21 pounds. Each large package weighs the same, and each small package weighs the same. What is the weight of 1 large package?

   _____

An *interjection* is a word or group of words that expresses emotion. An interjection should be followed by an exclamation point or a comma. Write an interjection to accompany each sentence. Then, write two additional sentences that include interjections and appropriate punctuation.

5. _____ That sauce is spicy!
6. _____ We arrived just in time.
7. _____ There is a rainbow!
8. _____ I left my lunch at home.

_____

_____

FITNESS FLASH: Put on your favorite song and have a dance party!

* See page ii.

DAY 5

Language Arts/Science

Figurative language refers to language that goes beyond the literal meaning of the words used. Writers use figurative language to convey meaning and to make their writing more interesting. *Metaphor, simile, hyperbole, personification, onomatopoeia,* and *oxymoron* are all examples of figurative language. Circle at least eight examples of figurative language in the paragraph below.

"Nat, you're pitching," Coach Adam says as he pats me on the back. It is the final inning of the game, and the score is tied, 2 to 2. As I jog out to the pitcher's mound, my mind is racing with all of the catastrophic ways this game could end. The baseball field is usually my sanctuary; but, at this moment, I do not feel safe at all. The first batter struts up to the plate, and as he takes his stance, my stomach drops like an out-of-control elevator. The batter, Jonah Watson, my archenemy since first grade, glares back at me like a tiger eyeing its prey. I just need to throw the first pitch, and then I know my nerves will vanish like dust in the air. My glove keeps my secret; I hold it up to cover my face. I do not want Jonah to see how nervous I am. He stands firmly in the batter's box, his long, silver bat taunting me as he tips it back and forth. I grip the ball and trace my fingers along the stitching. *I have done this a million times,* I assure myself. I am ready. I lift my leg, raise my arm, and let go. Smack. The ball flies by Jonah and hits the catcher's mitt. I hold my breath and wait for the umpire to make the call. After what feels like an eternity, she throws up her right hand. "Strike one!"

Label the steps of the food chain using the terms from the word bank.

| A. tertiary consumer | B. decomposer | C. primary consumer |
| D. secondary consumer | E. producer | |

9. _____ tree
10. _____ caterpillar eating the leaves of the tree
11. _____ bird eating the caterpillar
12. _____ snake eating the bird
13. _____ worms breaking down the dead organic matter when a snake dies
14. Explain where producers get their energy:

_____

_____

_____

108
© Carson Dellosa Education

Geometry/Grammar

DAY 6

Solve each problem. Round answers to the nearest tenth as needed.

1. Rosalia rides her bike south on Vintner Street for 30 meters. She then turns and rides her bike east on Miller Street. She ends up 226 meters away from where she began. How many meters did she ride east on Miller Street?

    _____

2. Jesper makes a pillow with triangular pattern blocks of fabric. Each pattern block is in the shape of a right triangle with two shorter sides that are each 4 inches long. What is the length of the third side?

    _____

3. The roof of a model tower is in the shape of a square pyramid with a height of 6 centimeters. The base has side lengths of 5 centimeters. What is the slant height of the roof?

    _____

Read the paragraph. There are ten grammar, punctuation, capitalization, and spelling errors. Identify and correct each one.

The Nazca Lines are a mysterius collection of giant figures drawn on a dessert plain about 250 miles South of Lima, Peru. The drawings, which are over 2,000 years old, includes straight lines geometric shapes, and giant animals, such as a spider, a monkey, and a duck. The figures are so large that they can only be seen from the air. Archeologists today wondered why they were made? Are they part of a Ceremony asking the gods for rain? Were they an astronomical calendar? We will probably never solve the mystery, of the Nazca Lines.

> **CHARACTER CHECK:** Think of a gift you can give someone that does not cost any money.

DAY 6

Reading Comprehension

Read the passage. Then, answer the questions.

The Appalachian Trail

The Appalachian Trail, at over 2,180 miles, stretches along the crest of the Appalachian Mountains, from Springer Mountain in Georgia to Mount Katahdin in Maine. This highly popular trail was the idea of Benton MacKaye, who first began to push for such an ambitious footpath in 1921. MacKaye believed that people would strongly benefit from more exposure to nature. He wrote, "Life for two weeks on the mountain top would show up many things about life during the other fifty weeks down below. The latter could be viewed as a whole—away from its heat, and sweat, and irritations. There would be a chance to catch a breath, to study the dynamic forces of nature and the possibilities of shifting to them the burdens now carried on the backs of men."

In 1923, the first section of the trail was built. It was completed in 1937, becoming the first footpath of the National Trail System. It was a promise of an easy way to enjoy nature for those who just want to hike a portion of the path. It was also a challenge for those who wanted to try to walk the whole thing. This was first done in 1948 by Earl Shaffer; and, since then, the path has provided a challenge for thousands of other hikers.

Over the decades, the Appalachian Trail has grown in popularity. This was magnified by the coronavirus pandemic, which began in 2020. People were looking for more outdoor activities as an escape from lockdowns. It is estimated that 3 million people hike at least a portion of the trail per year. This has led to overuse of the trail, including vandalism of hiking shelters and flagrant disregard of trail rules about pets and alcohol use. It seems that the peaceful solitude of nature, the ideals of which were professed by MacKaye, has become endangered by its own popularity.

4. Why did MacKaye want to construct the Appalachian Trail?
   A. for economic growth
   B. for an escape from life's problems
   C. for the challenge it provided
   D. for the promotion of his ideas

5. How do you think MacKaye might react to the popularity of the Appalachian Trail today?

   _____

   _____

6. Why is the Appalachian Trail considered part of the National Trail System?

   _____

   _____

CHARACTER CHECK: What can you do to show respect for nature?

Algebra/Vocabulary

DAY 7

For each system of equations, decide whether the system has *one solution*, *no solutions*, or *infinitely many solutions*.

1. $y - 2x = 1$ and $4y + 12x = -12$

   _____

2. $3y - 9x = 12$ and $y - 3x = -2$

   _____

3. $y + 4x = -1$ and $2y - 8x = -2$

   _____

4. $y - x = 2$ and $4y - 4x = 8$

   _____

5. $2y - 6x = 10$ and $y - 4x = -2$

   _____

6. $y - 5x = -3$ and $3y - 15x = -9$

   _____

Write the letter of the word from the word bank that correctly completes each sentence.

| A. wretched | B. fumigate | C. adhere | D. diplomacy | E. porous |

7. They had to _____ the shed when they discovered it had termites.
8. The politician was famous for her _____, so she was a natural choice for ambassador to the United Nations.
9. Joe felt _____ after the sculpture fell off the shelf and broke into pieces.
10. Since the counter was very _____, it absorbed the smell of whatever I cleaned it with.
11. If you attend Westlake High School, then you will have to _____ to the very strict dress code.

FACTOID: Most baby giraffes are about six feet tall at birth.

DAY 7

Reading Comprehension

Read the passage. Then, answer the questions.

The Mystery of Stonehenge

One of history's most enduring mysteries are the monoliths of Stonehenge. Located in the Salisbury Plain in England, this large circle of stones was erected some 4,600 years ago. Composed of immense sandstone blocks weighing 25 tons, Stonehenge is known throughout the world. What is not known, however, is why it was built.

Experts have long debated what Stonehenge was. Some of the more outlandish myths say that the wizard Merlin built it with the help of giants. More recent speculation even gives credit to ancient aliens for building Stonehenge as a landing place for spacecraft.

More reasonable theories state that Stonehenge may have been built for one of two purposes: Stonehenge was probably a spiritual site at which astronomical phenomena were observed. The monument is clearly aligned with the sun and moon. The site also could have been a monument to the wealth and power of ancient chieftains, since there are burial remains at Stonehenge. Perhaps Stonehenge served a combination of these purposes. Regardless, what is clear is that the mystery of Stonehenge will never be solved.

12. What evidence supports the theory that Stonehenge was used for astronomy?
    - A. burial remains
    - B. placement of stones
    - C. stone blocks
    - D. age of monument

13. How would a site such as Stonehenge have helped ancient chieftains show their power?

    _____

    _____

14. How are the theories about Stonehenge that involve Merlin and aliens connected?

    _____

    _____

FACTOID: Did you know that cows have four stomachs?

Algebra/Vocabulary

DAY 8

Factor the following quadratic equations into binomials.

1. $x^2 - 3x - 10 =$ _____

2. $y^2 + 15y + 56 =$ _____

3. $z^2 - 6z + 9 =$ _____

4. $a^2 + \dfrac{7}{6}a + \dfrac{1}{3} =$ _____

5. $10b^2 - 23b - 99 =$ _____

6. $-80c + 28c + 24 =$ _____

7. $81m^2 + 18m + 1 =$ _____

8. $-\dfrac{1}{2}n^2 + \dfrac{25}{2}n - 12 =$ _____

Look up each word in an online or print dictionary. Circle the syllable that is stressed. Then, write the word's part of speech and definition on the line. If it has more than one definition and part of speech, use the first one listed.

9. amorphous _____

10. ethereal _____

11. insatiable _____

12. longevity _____

13. preclude _____

14. subterfuge _____

15. zealous _____

© Carson Dellosa Education

DAY 8

Read each word. Write the root word, the prefix, and the suffix in the correct columns. Some words will have either a prefix or a suffix, and some words may have both a prefix and a suffix.

		Prefix	Root Word	Suffix
16.	maladjustment			
17.	dissimilar			
18.	characterize			
19.	reformatory			
20.	commentary			

The Guinness Book of World Records is a book (and website) that has been verifying and recording world records since 1955. There are a large variety of records included: longest fingernails, oldest person, most consecutive cartwheels completed, etc. Think of a world record that you would be interested in achieving and describe it below. Also, include how you would go about achieving this record. Use an additional sheet of paper if needed.

_____

_____

_____

_____

_____

_____

FITNESS FLASH: Look up what "child's pose" is and hold this pose for 30 seconds.

* See page ii.

Geometry/Grammar

DAY 9

Find the distance between the two points given. Round your answer to two decimal places.

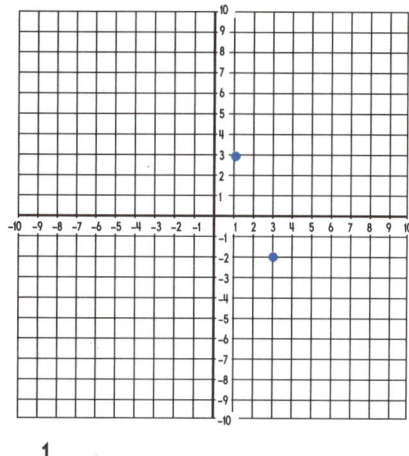
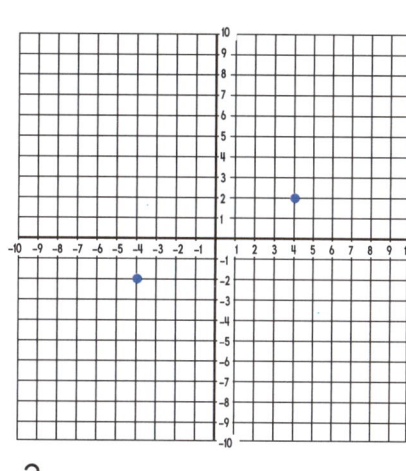
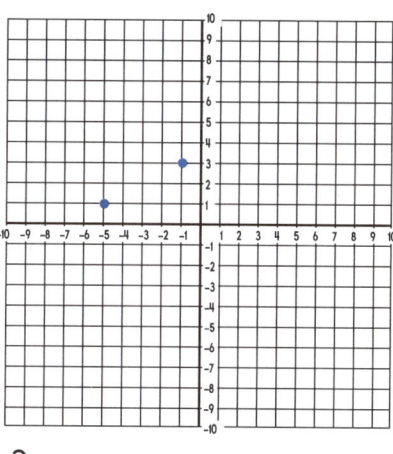

1. _____   2. _____   3. _____

When the subject of a sentence performs the action, the verb is in the *active voice*. When the subject of a sentence is being acted upon, the verb is in the *passive voice*. It is appropriate to use the passive voice in the following cases: (1) to focus attention on the action in a sentence rather than on who is doing the action; (2) when the person doing the action is unknown or does not matter; and (3) in academic or scientific writing.

Read each sentence. Each one is written with a verb in the passive voice. Write *PV* on the line if the passive voice is appropriate. If passive voice is not appropriate, then rewrite the sentence using active voice.

4. President Johnson was sworn in as president of the United States on Air Force One. _____

5. Thirty pages of the history textbook were read by Jamie last night. _____

6. When I got back to my parking space, I discovered that my car was covered in snow. _____

7. Opening night of the play was postponed because the lead actor had laryngitis. _____

8. The ceiling and the walls were painted by my mother. _____

9. Three beakers were filled with an acidic solution, and three were filled with a basic solution. _____

DAY 9

Reading Comprehension/Science

Read the poem. Then, answer the questions.

But Outer Space By Robert Frost

But outer Space, 1
At least this far,
For all the fuss
Of the populace

Stays more popular 5
Than populous

10. What is the meaning of this poem?
    A. Outer space is popular to discuss, but not widely visited.
    B. Outer space is neither widely discussed nor visited.
    C. Travel to outer space has not been achieved.
    D. Travel to outer space is regularly achieved.

11. Which line contains a word meaning people in a community?
    A. 2
    B. 3
    C. 4
    D. 5

12. What are the last words in lines 4 and 6 called?
    A. homonyms
    B. homophones
    C. onomatopoeia
    D. simile

Look at the list of changes provided. Sort the changes into two categories: chemical or physical.

- cracking an egg
- mixing cake batter
- boiling water
- baking a cake
- steeping tea leaves
- combining vinegar and milk to make buttermilk
- cooling tea with ice
- lighting a campfire
- roasting a marshmallow
- sandwiching chocolate and a marshmallow between graham crackers

Chemical	Physical

Geometry/Grammar

DAY 10

Solve each problem. Use 3.14 for π. Round your answers to the nearest tenth as needed. Show your work on a separate sheet of paper.

1. A cylindrical block of wood in a children's toy set has a height of 5 centimeters. The base has a radius of 2 centimeters. What is the volume of wood in this cylindrical block?

    _____

2. The base radius of a cylinder is 3 feet. The height of the cylinder is 5.75 feet. What is the volume of the cylinder?

    _____

3. A section of a cylindrical pipe has an inside diameter of 1.5 inches and a length of 7 inches. What is the largest volume of water that can flow through this section of the pipe at a given time?

    _____

4. A cylinder has a base area of 36.8 centimeters squared and a height of 4 centimeters. What is the volume of the cylinder?

    _____

A *relative pronoun* begins a relative clause. Four relative pronouns are *who*, *whom*, *that*, and *which*. *Who* and *whom* are used to refer to people. *Who* is used as the subject of a relative clause; *whom* is used as the object of a relative clause. *That* and *which* are used to refer to objects or ideas. *That* is used when the information in the relative clause is needed in the sentence; *which* is used when the information in the relative clause is not needed in the sentence. Read each sentence. Then, write the correct relative pronoun in the blank.

5. The novel *War and Peace*, _____ I want to read next summer, is over 1,000 pages long.
6. I asked the electrician _____ was fixing the air conditioner if it would be working soon.
7. The man _____ sang "The Star-Spangled Banner" at the baseball game is my music teacher.
8. The box of canned goods _____ is in the trunk should be dropped off at the food pantry.
9. Mrs. Adlow, _____ we met last summer, will be the new principal of our school.
10. I promise I will never tell anyone the secret _____ you shared with me.

DAY 10

Literary Terms/Science

Write the letter of the term from the word bank that matches each definition.

A. irony	B. satire	C. rhetorical question	D. author's voice	E. style

11. _____ the personality of an author that comes through in his or her writing
12. _____ the use of language that says the opposite of what is really meant
13. _____ the specific way in which an author writes
14. _____ the use of humor or exaggeration to point out the faults of a person or group
15. _____ the question an author uses to get readers to think about a topic

Read each description, and choose the corresponding object from the word bank that matches each description. Objects may match multiple descriptions.

textbook	water
helium gas	lemonade
oxygen gas	pencil

16. maintains shape even when placed into a backpack _____
17. takes the shape of a glass _____
18. has a freezing point of 0°C and a boiling point of 100°C _____
19. density is less than that of air found in the troposphere; will float _____
20. often composed of wood, metal, graphite, and rubber _____
21. reacts with metals to rust their surfaces _____

FACTOID: One day on Venus is longer than an entire year on Earth.

Geometry/Writing

DAY 11

Solve each problem using the formula for the volume of a cone: $V = \frac{1}{3}\pi r^2 h$, or $V = \frac{1}{3}bh$. Use 3.14 as the value of π. Round to the nearest tenth and include the correct units of measure.

1. What is the volume of a cone with a height of 3 centimeters and a radius of 4 centimeters?

   _____

2. A conical holding tank has a diameter of 18 feet and a height of 22 feet. How much water can this tank hold?

   _____

3. How much ice cream will fit in an ice cream cone that measures 3 inches across the widest part of the top, and is 5 inches tall?

   _____

4. Find the volume of a cone with a height of 7.1 meters and a base area of 28.27 meters squared.

   _____

5. A cone is 38 inches tall and has a volume of 2,850 inches cubed. What is the radius?

   _____

6. A vase has a cone-shaped bowl that rests on a solid glass stem and base. The cone has a slant height of 10 centimeters and a radius of 6 centimeters. How many of these vases could be filled to the brim with a 2-liter bottle of water? (1 liter = 1,000 cm³)

   _____

Imagine what it might be like to wake up one morning and have the ability to foresee the future. Do you think this would be a gift or a curse? Provide at least one example of how this would be beneficial and one example of how it would be negative.

_____

_____

_____

_____

_____

DAY 11

Reading Comprehension

Read the passage. Then, answer the questions.

The Life of Beverly Cleary

At one time or another in your childhood, you might have read a book by Beverly Cleary. Maybe you have even seen one of the movies made from her books. This popular children's author brought to life characters such as Ramona Quimby; Ramona's sister, Beezus; Henry Huggins; and Ralph S. Mouse.

Beverly Cleary was born in Oregon in 1916 and lived to be 104. She struggled with school and reading as a very young child, but she soon improved and grew passionate about reading and writing. This led her to a college degree in English and then to a career as a librarian.

Cleary's first book was *Henry Huggins*, and it was published in 1950. This was followed by *Beezus and Ramona* in 1955. Cleary's books were based on the lives of young characters and humorous situations in their day-to-day lives. Ramona, the **precocious** lead, became so beloved that Cleary ended up writing three additional titles about her. Cleary's books provide a blend of humor with some teachable moments for addressing issues that young children may face, including the divorce of parents, moving, and a parent's loss of a job.

Cleary's books seem to be timeless, entertaining current generations as much as they have previous generations.

7. What genre best describes Cleary's books?
   - A. nonfiction
   - B. historical fiction
   - C. realistic fiction
   - D. fantasy

8. How many books did Cleary write about Ramona in all?
   - A. one
   - B. two
   - C. three
   - D. four

9. Which word best defines *precocious*?
   - A. disobedient
   - B. playful
   - C. adorable
   - D. clever

10. Have you read any of Beverly Cleary's books? If so, which ones? If not, which sound interesting to you? _____

Geometry/Parts of Speech

DAY 12

Find the volume of each sphere described. Recall that the volume is equal to $\frac{4}{3}\pi r^3$ and the surface area is equal to $4\pi r^2$. Round to the nearest hundredth if necessary.

1. A sphere has a diameter of 16 feet.
   The volume of the sphere is
   _____

2. A sphere has a radius of 3.2 meters.
   The volume of the sphere is
   _____

3. A sphere has a surface area of 144π centimeters squared.
   The volume of the sphere is
   _____

4. At its widest point, a spherical ball measures 8 inches across.
   The volume of the ball is
   _____

5. A spherical spore has a radius of 5 micrometers.
   The volume of the spore is
   _____

6. A spherical valve has a diameter of 6 inches.
   The volume of the valve is
   _____

The *subject* of a sentence is the person or thing that is doing the action in the sentence. The *direct object* is the person or thing that is acted upon in the sentence. Read each sentence. Then, underline the subject once and the direct object twice.

7. Adriana sold six quilts at the craft fair last month.
8. My mother finally completed her jigsaw puzzle.
9. Carson will play "Moonlight Sonata" at his piano recital.
10. The detective examined the footprint with his magnifying glass.
11. Monique read "Hansel and Gretel" to her little sister.
12. I asked Tyler to help me with my math homework.
13. The chef sprinkled chopped parsley over the chicken stew.
14. We watched *The Lion King* last Friday night.

FITNESS FLASH: Run for 30 seconds, walk for 30 seconds, and then run as fast as you can for 15 seconds.

* See page ii.

DAY 12

Reading Comprehension

Read the passage. Then, answer the questions.

Emperor Penguins

The largest known penguin species, growing up to 45 inches tall, is the Emperor penguin (scientific name *Aptenodytes forsteri*). There are 18 total penguin species, and the closest relative to the Emperor penguin is the King penguin (scientific name *Aptenodytes patagonicus*). The genus name *Aptenodytes* comes from a Greek word meaning "featherless diver." That name suits the Emperor penguin quite well, as these birds can dive up to 1,850 feet down into the freezing waters near Antarctica. During their dives, adult penguins search for fish, squid, or krill.

Emperor penguins have many unique adaptations that allow them to breed during the harsh winters of their habitat, usually between the months of June through September. The female penguin will lay a single egg and then leave this egg to be incubated by the male penguin using the warmth of his brood pouch, a layer of feathered skin near the feet. The female penguin leaves shortly after laying the egg to make the long journey to the sea to find food to bring back to her chick. The male penguins remain with their colony and form huddles for warmth. The males take turns being on the outside of the huddle, where the harsh winds can be difficult to endure. The male penguins are also fasting during the incubation period, and will not be able to leave for food until their partners return from the sea. The female penguins return from their hunt, sometimes after several months, with a stomach full of food to be shared with the chick.

Climate change is proving to be a major threat to the survival of the Emperor penguin. This penguin's breeding grounds are melting in the world's warmer temperatures, and the birds may soon run out of space.

15. Which of the following best explains why the genus name *Aptenodytes* suits the Emperor penguin?
    A. The penguins only lay one egg.
    B. The penguins huddle together for warmth.
    C. The penguins dive deep into the ocean to obtain food.
    D. The penguins breed between the months of June and September.

16. Among Emperor penguins, who is responsible for the incubation of the egg?
    A. the male penguin
    B. the female penguin
    C. both the male and the female penguins
    D. neither parent, as they bury the egg in the ground

17. List some adaptations that have allowed penguins to survive in the freezing temperatures of Antarctica. _____
    _____
    _____

Algebra/Language Arts

DAY 13

Find the vertex of each quadratic function.

1. $y = x^2 - 4x + 2$

2. $y = x^2 + 6x - 4$

3. $y = 2x^2 - 3x + 6$

4. $y = -x^2 + 8x - 10$

Identify the axis of symmetry for each quadratic equation.

5. $y = x^2 - 4x - 45$

6. $y = 2x^2 + 6x - 9$

Texts can be structured in a variety of ways to help provide the reader with a better overall understanding of the information.

Read each text summary, and write which type of text organization is used: *chronological*, *cause/effect*, *problem/solution*, *descriptive*, *compare/contrast*, or *sequence*.

7. In March 1861, Abraham Lincoln became president of the United States. He issued the Emancipation Proclamation in 1863, declaring freedom for enslaved people. He was re-elected as president in 1864, but he was assassinated in 1865.

8. To make pancake batter, first gather all of your ingredients, a mixing bowl, and a whisk. Next, combine and stir all of the dry ingredients together. Then, add the wet ingredients and whisk until all lumps have been removed. Finally, your batter is ready for the griddle.

9. There were many differences between the book and the movie based on the book. The characters, setting, and the basic plot were the same in both, but there were many details left out of the movie, such as the secret passageway that was used for getting in and going out of the building undetected.

10. Ring-tailed lemurs are a mammal species native only to Madagascar, an island of Africa. Adult lemurs are small, often weighing 6 pounds or less, with a tail that can be as long as 2 feet. The lemurs have 13 black-and-white rings around their long tails.

DAY 13

Science/Character Development

Read the list of energy resources provided in the word bank. Sort the resources into two categories: renewable and non-renewable.

Energy Resources

| biomass | geothermal | natural gas | petroleum/oil | wood/timber |
| coal | hydropower/water | nuclear | wind (turbines) | solar |

Renewable	Non-renewable

Respect

The Dalai Lama said, "Follow three rules: respect yourself, respect others, and take responsibility for all your actions." This is important advice to live by.

What does it look like to respect yourself? You should have confidence in yourself, be proud of who you are, and take care of yourself. Self-respect involves ensuring that your body is healthy and rested and that you treat yourself in a positive way. It is important for you to first accept who you are and what makes you unique; once you find this self-acceptance, you will be able to show your true self to the world.

Respecting others is important as it shows someone that you value them and what they say or think. Show respect by being a good and supportive listener. Treat people with kindness and be polite. You may have different opinions or beliefs than other people, but it is important to respect those differences.

Take responsibility for your actions. Everyone makes mistakes. This is part of life and is unavoidable. However, the way in which you handle your mistakes is important. If you do something wrong, admit it and learn from your error. This is how you grow. Being able to take responsibility for your actions and admit your mistakes will lead to respect from others.

FACTOID: A certain species of bamboo can grow up to 35 inches in a single day.

Data Analysis

DAY 14

Determine whether each scatterplot shows a *positive correlation*, a *negative correlation*, or *no correlation* between x and y.

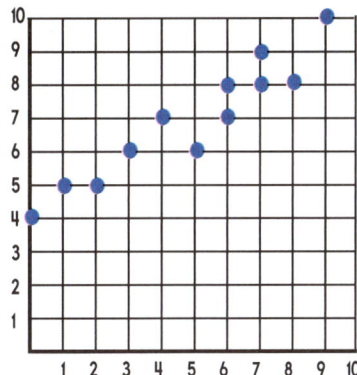 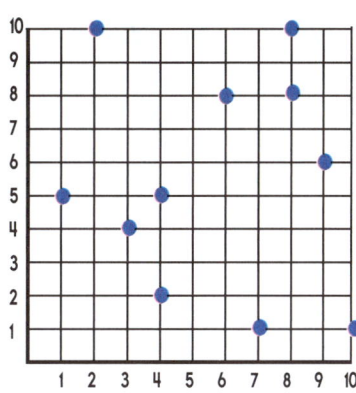 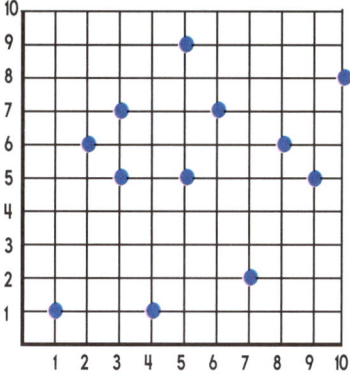

1. _____ 2. _____ 3. _____

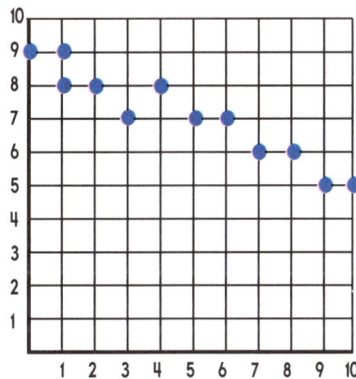 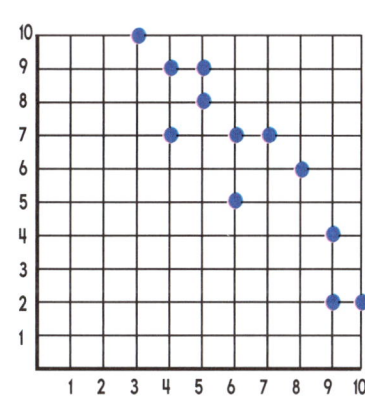 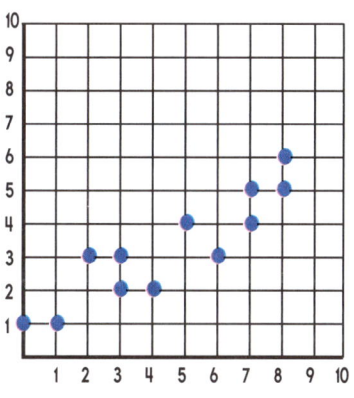

4. _____ 5. _____ 6. _____

CHARACTER CHECK: Think about someone you admire. What do you admire about this person?

DAY 14

Literary Terms

Logos, ethos, and pathos are the three main types of persuasive strategies used in arguments. *Logos* relies on logic or reason to convince an audience. *Pathos* appeals to an audience's emotions or feelings. *Ethos* is based on the reliability of the writer or speaker. Read each passage and answer the question that follows.

7. Reading is a great way to broaden your vocabulary. Starting in kindergarten, if a student reads 20 minutes a day at home, they will hear 1.8 million words per year, and by sixth grade they will have read for 851 hours. Reading new words in many different contexts gives you a deeper understanding of these words, so you will become more proficient at using them in your own speaking and writing.

   What persuasive strategy does the writer use in this passage? Explain how you know.

   _____

8. Is there anything better than cozying up with your baby and sharing a story together? Reading to young children can do two things: teach your child to love reading, and improve family relationships. Young children like nothing more than to spend time with their families. Reading with your young child each day can actually make them like reading more as an older child, because reading is tied to one of their favorite childhood memories: spending time with their mom or dad.

   What persuasive strategy does the writer use in this passage? Explain how you know.

   _____

9. After teaching kindergarten for twenty-five years, I have seen firsthand the benefits of reading at home. My students who spent the most time reading both at school and at home had stronger vocabularies, improved memories, and excellent spelling skills. Furthermore, I would always tell my students that the more books we read, the more worlds we are exposed to outside of our own.

   What persuasive strategy does the writer use in this passage? Explain how you know.

   _____

CHARACTER CHECK: How can a person prove that they are a trustworthy friend?

Functions/Vocabulary

DAY 15

Determine whether each function is *increasing* or *decreasing*.

1. $y = 4x - 4$

   _____

2. $10x + y = 20$

   _____

3. $y = -0.5x + 7$

   _____

4. $9x - 3y = -3$

   _____

5. $y = 9x$

   _____

6. $y = 5.75 - 8x$

   _____

7. $y - 3 = 2x$

   _____

8. $-2y = -12x + 14$

   _____

9. $-\frac{3}{8}x = y$

   _____

10. $y = \frac{1}{2} + 3x$

    _____

Circle the answer that correctly completes each analogy.

11. impulsive : spontaneous :: _____
    - A. audible : silent
    - B. dauntless : brave
    - C. complex : simple
    - D. indelible : temporary

12. antagonize : help :: _____
    - A. delete : erase
    - B. concede : accept
    - C. terminate : end
    - D. compress : expand

13. celebrity : famous :: _____
    - A. actor : movies
    - B. desert : arid
    - C. heathen : religious
    - D. sharp : bayonet

14. stratus : cloud :: _____
    - A. tree : maple
    - B. tornado : hurricane
    - C. velociraptor : dinosaur
    - D. prehistoric : medieval

15. mortify : embarrass :: _____
    - A. ravage : damage
    - B. complaint : tantrum
    - C. tolerate : love
    - D. dwindle : shrink

16. whittler : knife :: _____
    - A. scalpel : surgeon
    - B. gardener : flowers
    - C. conductor : saxophone
    - D. archaeologist : trowel

DAY 15

Reading Comprehension

Read the passage. Then, answer the questions.

Katherine Johnson

As a mathematician, a NASA scientist, and a Black woman, Katherine Johnson opened doors of opportunity that had never been opened before. Johnson was born on August 26, 1918, in West Virginia, at a time when Black women were not often afforded many opportunities. Katherine always excelled at math and earned a B.S. in Mathematics and French. She worked as a teacher for many years.

In 1953, Johnson was made aware of an opportunity to work for NACA (National Advisory Committee for Aeronautics), which later became NASA (National Aeronautics and Space Administration). She began working in the West Area Computer Department, and her exceptional calculation skills did not go unnoticed. She was quickly promoted to higher-level assignments. In 1961, she analyzed the trajectory for Alan Shepard's mission, Freedom 7, the first human space flight successfully conducted by the United States. Because of her work on Shepard's mission, John Glenn asked that she also check his numbers for his 1962 orbital mission.

Throughout her time at NASA, Johnson authored and co-authored 26 research reports, the first of which was published in 1960 and co-authored with Ted Skopinski. Johnson was the first woman to receive credit for a research report within the Flight Research Division. Because of her many contributions to space science and orbital calculations, Katherine Johnson was awarded the Presidential Medal of Freedom in 2015 by President Barack Obama. Johnson passed away on February 24, 2020.

17. Why was Katherine Johnson's report that was co-authored with Skopinski so groundbreaking?
    A. It marked Johnson's first real accomplishment.
    B. It was the first time Johnson was asked to work for NACA.
    C. It was the first time Johnson knew she wanted to explore space.
    D. It was the first time a woman had been given author credit within the Flight Research Division.

18. What was Johnson's first assignment at NACA/NASA?
    A. working with the Flight Research Division
    B. calculating the numbers for John Glenn's orbit
    C. working with the West Area Computer Department
    D. calculating the numbers for Alan Shepard's orbit

19. Who awarded Katherine Johnson the Presidential Medal of Freedom? Underline his name in the text.

Data Analysis/Language Arts

DAY 16

Compare the values of the data represented in each misleading graph.

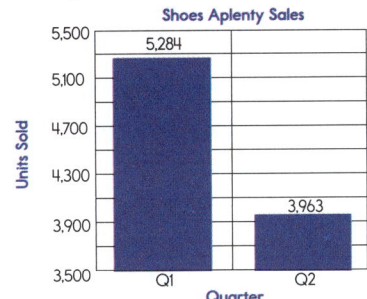

1. The second bar is less than one-third the height of the first bar. In reality, sales decreased by what fraction between quarter one and quarter two at Shoes Aplenty?

   _____

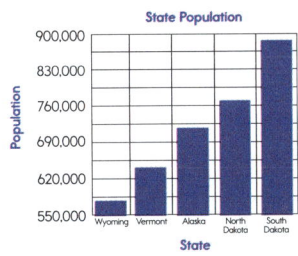

2. The graph shows the populations of the five least populous U.S. states. The graph makes it appear that the population of South Dakota is about ten times that of Wyoming. The actual ratio of the population of South Dakota to the population of Wyoming is closer to what?

   _____

3. Use the graph from question 2 to compare the populations of two other states.

   _____

Alliteration is the repetition of consonant sounds at the beginnings of nearby words. *Onomatopoeia* is the use of a word that sounds like the noise it describes. Read each sentence. Write *A* if the sentence contains alliteration. Write *O* if the sentence contains onomatopoeia.

4. _____ The bookcase tottered over and then crashed onto the floor.
5. _____ The white noise machine made a soft, soothing sound that helped me sleep.
6. _____ The buzzing fly circled the tray of fruit on the picnic table.
7. _____ The bluebird beat its wings and flew away.
8. _____ The fireworks whizzed into the sky and exploded with a boom.
9. _____ I was woken up from my nap by the clanging of the doorbell.

DAY 16

Reading Comprehension/Science

Read the passage. Then, answer the questions.

Daedalus and Icarus

King Minos of Crete imprisoned the architect Daedalus and his son Icarus on an island. One day, as Daedalus stood on the shore and watched the birds, he thought of a way that he and Icarus could escape. He collected feathers and used wax and thread to **fashion** them into two sets of wings. He then taught himself and Icarus how to use the wings so they could fly off the island to freedom. "But you must be sure," he told his son, "not to fly too close to the sun. The heat will melt the wax, and the wings will fall apart." Icarus promised his father he would not fly too high, but once he felt the thrill of rushing through the air, he flew higher and higher and would not listen to his father's cries. There was nothing Daedalus could do as he watched Icarus's wings droop and his son plunge into the sea. Today, we call the sea that Icarus supposedly fell into the Icarian Sea.

10. What is the theme of the passage?
    A. It is important to have self-control.
    B. Animals can teach humans a lot about life.
    C. Some rules are too difficult to follow.
    D. There is often conflict between fathers and sons.

11. Which of the following words best defines the word *fashion* as it is used in the passage?
    A. dress   B. look   C. make   D. style

12. How are Daedalus and Icarus different from each other?

_____

_____

Complete the Punnett square and answer the questions.

In this genetic cross, *R* represents the dominant trait for round peas, and *r* represents the recessive trait for wrinkled peas.

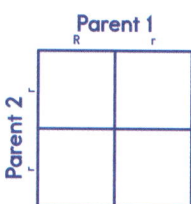

13. Possible genotypes for the offspring produced in this cross:

_____

14. Possible phenotypes for the offspring produced in this cross:

_____

15. Percentage of offspring that will have round peas:

_____

16. Percentage of offspring that will have wrinkled peas:

_____

Geometry/Writing

DAY 17

Solve each problem. Use 3.14 for π. Write your answer as a decimal number.

1. The top part of Theresa's model rocket is shaped like a cone. The cone is 6 centimeters long, and the base of the cone has a radius of 2 centimeters. Find the volume of the cone with the formula $V = \pi r^2 \frac{h}{3}$

   _____ cm³

2. A globe in a library is shaped like a sphere with a radius of 6 inches. Find the volume of the sphere with the formula $V = \frac{4}{3}\pi r^3$

   _____ in.³

3. The trash can in Quan's office is shaped like a cylinder with a height of 32 inches and a radius of 9 inches. Find the volume of the cylinder with the formula $V = \pi r^2 h$

   _____ in.³

As you get closer to the first day of school, consider what you are most excited about in this upcoming school year and what you are least excited about. Write your responses below. Use another piece of paper if you need more space.

_____
_____
_____
_____
_____
_____
_____
_____

CHARACTER CHECK: Write about a time when you showed courage.

DAY 17

Language Arts/Fitness

Paraphrasing is an important skill in language arts. It is when you use your own words to restate someone else's ideas without changing the original intent of the message. When paraphrasing, it is important to cite the original source and be sure that you are not plagiarizing, or copying word for word, the content. Practice by paraphrasing the given passage.

When learning to drive, it is imperative to be safe. Seat belts should always be buckled upon entering a vehicle, and then all mirrors should be checked and adjusted as needed. It is crucial to be aware of your surroundings before you turn the car on and move from the parked position.

_____
_____
_____
_____
_____
_____

Pickleball

Have you heard of the latest fitness craze called pickleball? Pickleball is a blend of tennis, badminton, and table tennis. It can be played either indoors or outdoors using a tennis net. An official pickleball court uses a tennis net with modifications, and the court is the same size as a badminton court. The equipment includes a paddle and a plastic ball with holes. The paddle is solid and is much smaller than a tennis racquet, but is slightly larger and more rectangular than a table tennis paddle.

The goal of pickleball is similar to that of tennis and table tennis: players are trying to score on the opposing team by hitting the ball over the net with no return on their volley.

While pickleball has recently been increasing in popularity, with designated pickleball courts and facilities popping up around the country, it has actually been around since 1965, invented in Washington state by three dads trying to entertain their children. It is now achieving popularity in both the United States and Canada, as well as in some European countries.

If you have never played pickleball, then find a place near you that has equipment and give it a try. No pickles are needed.

Algebra/Language Arts

DAY 18

Use the graph to find the solution for each quadratic equation.

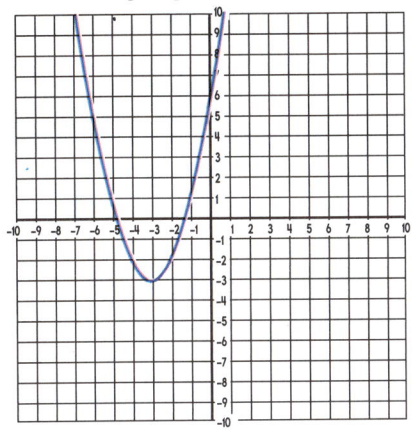 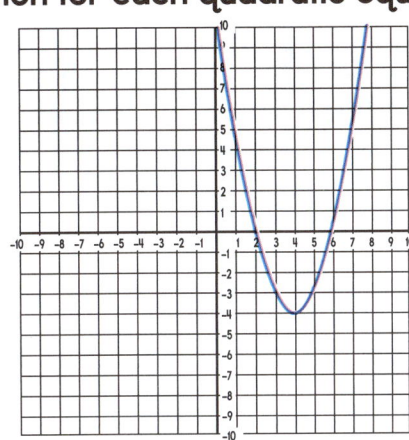 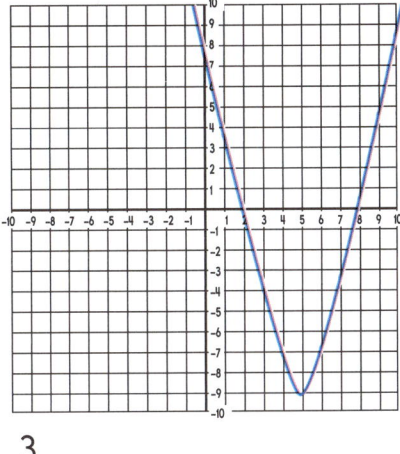

1. _____   2. _____   3. _____

Tell if the given value is a solution of the given equation. Explain your reasoning.

4. $y = x^2 - 3x - 28$, $x = 4$ _____

_____

5. $y = x^2 + 5x - 14$, $x = 7$ _____

_____

When an author writes, they are hoping to evoke a *mood* in their reader. Mood describes the feeling or ambience of a piece of writing. Read the sentences and identify the mood of the writing. Then, underline any words or phrases that contribute to that mood.

6. It was a dark and stormy night, and the crew members were alone in the darkness of the woods, with the nearest home several miles away.

   _____

7. Payal took a deep breath as she stared at the envelope from the university. Her stomach in knots, she slowly opened the envelope and unfolded the paper, squeezing her eyes shut.

   _____

8. She quickly got to her feet, cheeks burning, eyes stinging, and pushed through the throngs of people whom she was sure were pointing and laughing at her.

   _____

DAY 18

Reading Comprehension

Read the recipe. Then, answer the questions.

Chocolate Chip Cookies
(makes 4 dozen cookies)

Ingredients
- 4 cups flour
- $1\frac{1}{2}$ teaspoons baking soda
- $1\frac{1}{4}$ teaspoons salt
- $1\frac{1}{2}$ cups butter, softened
- $1\frac{1}{2}$ cups granulated sugar
- $\frac{3}{4}$ cup dark brown sugar, firmly packed
- 3 large eggs
- 3 teaspoons vanilla extract
- 1 bag (12 ounces) semisweet chocolate chips

Sift the flour, baking soda, and salt. Mix the butter and sugars. Add in the eggs and vanilla. Mix in the sifted dry ingredients. When blended, stir in the chocolate chips. Roll the dough into one-inch balls and place on a cookie sheet. Bake at 375°F for 8 minutes. Let the trays of cookies cool before eating.

9. For how long should you bake the cookies?
   - A. 4 minutes
   - B. 7 minutes
   - C. 8 minutes
   - D. 12 minutes

10. How many cookies does the recipe produce?
    - A. 4
    - B. 12
    - C. 16
    - D. 48

11. What is your favorite type of cookie? Do you prefer store-bought cookies or homemade? Why? _____
    _____
    _____

FACTOID: The world's largest chocolate chip cookie was made in 2003 and weighed 40,000 pounds.

Fractions & Decimals/Grammar

DAY 19

Write each fraction as a decimal value.

1. $\frac{17}{25}$ = _____
2. $\frac{3}{5}$ = _____
3. $\frac{244}{400}$ = _____
4. $\frac{15}{30}$ = _____
5. $\frac{114}{150}$ = _____
6. $\frac{234}{200}$ = _____
7. $\frac{275}{125}$ = _____
8. $\frac{45}{60}$ = _____

A *colon* (:) is used to introduce an item or a series of items. A colon is always used after a full sentence. A colon is never used with an introductory word or phrase. Read each sentence. Write C on the line if the colon is used correctly. Correct the error in the sentence if the colon is not used correctly.

9. _____ I will bring three things on our hike this afternoon: a rain jacket, a bag of trail mix, and a bottle of water.

10. _____ I have read many novels by Charles Dickens, including: *David Copperfield, A Tale of Two Cities, Oliver Twist,* and *A Christmas Carol.*

11. _____ After you mow the lawn: make sure to put the lawn mower back in the garden shed.

12. _____ One day I would like to travel to: the Pacific Ocean, the Gobi Desert, and the Himalayan Mountains.

13. _____ I learned a very important lesson when I built the doghouse: always measure before cutting.

14. _____ Only a few of my teachers didn't come to the opening night of the play: Mrs. Mead, Mr. Trainor, and Mr. Jarvis.

15. _____ You should watch some old black-and-white movies, for example: *Casablanca, It's a Wonderful Life,* and *The Philadelphia Story.*

FITNESS FLASH: Play catch with a friend and see how many consecutive catches you can make before missing one.

* See page ii.

Vocabulary/Language Arts

DAY 19

Use the context clues within the sentence to determine the meaning of the underlined term. Select the correct meaning.

16. Not wearing my glasses definitely impairs my vision.
    A. corrects
    B. diminishes
    C. harms
    D. improves

17. I have an amiable relationship with my neighbors, and we often play basketball together.
    A. competitive
    B. distant
    C. off-putting
    D. pleasant

18. The dog sat by the man's side, steadfast and unmoving, throughout the journey.
    A. contagious
    B. faithful
    C. sickly
    D. silent

19. The woman's vocation was accounting, even though she strongly disliked math.
    A. career
    B. hobby
    C. pastime
    D. talent

The *subject* of a sentence is the person or thing doing the action in a sentence. The *direct object* is the person or thing that is acted upon in the sentence. The *indirect object* precedes the direct object and indicates *to whom* or *for whom* the action of the verb is done.

Read each sentence. Then, underline the subject once and the direct object twice. Circle the indirect object if there is one.

20. Jason gave our dog a bath in the kitchen sink.
21. I read five books that were on the summer reading list.
22. My friends made me lasagna on my birthday.
23. Coach Johnson gave the team a pep talk before the championship game.
24. Laura won first prize in the science fair for her project on black holes.
25. We hung the family portrait between the two windows in the living room.
26. Tom gave the lilac bush plenty of water and plant food.
27. T.S. Eliot won the Nobel Prize for Literature in 1948.

Problem Solving/Grammar

DAY 20

Solve each problem. If needed, round to the nearest hundredth or cent.

1. Pamela buys groceries totaling $37.26 before tax. If the sales tax rate is 6%, what will the total charge be?

   _____

2. *The Daily Times* reports that 15% of its readership also reads a rival newspaper, *The Daily Herald*. *The Daily Herald* reports that 5,250 people read both newspapers. What is the total readership of *The Daily Times*?

   _____

3. Eduardo has a coupon for an extra 10% off for a luggage sale. The luggage is already on sale for 40% off, and then the coupon is applied to the discount price. A suitcase has a regular price of $59.99. What will be the price Eduardo pays after the discount and coupon?

   _____

4. Hamburgers Plus has a 10% discount on their french fries before 4:00 pm. Jamal goes there for lunch and buys the following items: a hamburger (regular price: $4.99), fries (regular price: $2.49), and a soda (regular price: $1.49). Sales tax is 7.5% and is applied after any discounts. What will Jamal's total be with the discount on fries, plus sales tax?

   _____

An *appositive* is a noun, a pronoun, or a noun phrase that usually follows another noun or pronoun and describes it. The appositive is set off by commas. A *main clause* has a subject and a verb, and it expresses a complete thought. A *subordinate clause* has a subject and a verb but does not express a complete thought.
Read the pair of sentences.

Pride and Prejudice is my favorite novel. *Pride and Prejudice* was written more than 200 years ago.

5. Combine the pair of sentences so that the new sentence has an appositive. Underline the appositive. _____

   _____

6. Combine the pair of sentences so that the new sentence has a main clause and a subordinate clause. Underline the subordinate clause. _____

   _____

DAY 20

Critical Thinking/Social Studies

Several friends all have different types of transportation: a bicycle, a golf cart, roller skates, a scooter (three-wheeled), and a skateboard. Use the information and deductive reasoning to determine which form of transportation belongs to each friend.

- Jade's and Brenna's forms of transportation use four wheels.
- Both Brenna and Tony use their feet to push off from the street when they ride their forms of transportation.
- Finn's form of transportation has the most wheels.
- Tiana's form of transportation has the fewest wheels.

	Bicycle	Golf cart	Roller skates	Scooter	Skateboard
Jade		X			
Brenna					X
Finn			X		
Tiana	X				
Tony				X	

Write the word from the word bank to correctly complete each sentence.

| suffrage | elections | race | sex | poll taxes | eighteen |

7. Citizens vote for candidates for office during _____.

8. The Twenty-Fourth Amendment prohibited the use of _____ as a way to stop people from voting.

9. _____, or the right to vote, was denied to women and African Americans early in the United States' history.

10. The Nineteenth Amendment prohibited states from denying people the right to vote based on _____.

11. After the Vietnam War, the Twenty-Sixth Amendment allowed people _____ years and older to vote.

12. The Fifteenth Amendment, passed after the Civil War, allowed people of any _____ to vote.

Science Experiment

Monitoring the Weather

Let's measure and record the daily temperature and the wind strength in your location using a wind vane. These recordings should be completed at the same time every day.

Materials:

- outdoor thermometer
- used plastic grocery bags
- scissors
- empty plastic water or soda bottle
- hook
- string

Procedure:

Cut a 1"- to 2"-wide ring from the plastic bottle (with adult help if needed). Then, cut 1"-wide strips out of the plastic bags.

Fold the plastic bag strips in half, making a loop at one end. Wrap the plastic bag strips around the plastic bottle ring, threading the tails of the plastic bag through the loop and pulling tight to secure the strips. Repeat this step with all of the plastic bag strips until the bottle ring is covered.

Tie each end of the string around the bottle ring so it can be hung. Hang the wind vane on a hook making sure the area is exposed so it can be blown around.

Day	Time	Hours of daylight	Temperature (°F)	Wind Direction	Wind Speed (low, medium, high)	Weather Conditions
1						
2						
3						
4						
5						
6						
7						

Use a computer to look up the time of sunrise and sunset in your area to calculate how many hours of daylight you received.

1. Is there a relationship between the temperature and the number of hours of daylight? Why or why not? _____

2. Is there a relationship between the wind speed and the temperature? Explain.

Science Experiment

BONUS

Balloon Rockets
What forces cause a rocket to launch?
When a rocket launches into space, the force of the thrust pushing out of the rocket's engine and against the air behind the rocket allows the rocket to move forward. In this experiment, you will use air pushing against air to create thrust. Your rocket will travel on a straw suspended on a string. You will see if the length of the straw has any impact on the distance the rocket can travel.

Materials:
- string or yarn
- balloon
- straw
- masking tape
- ruler
- scissors

Procedure:
1. Determine where you will tie your string for support. Chairs, doorknobs, or under piles of heavy books are all great places.
2. Attach one end of the string to the first support.
3. Thread the straw through the string and secure the second end of the string to the second support.
4. Blow up the balloon, but do not tie the end.
5. Tape the balloon to the straw in two places.
6. Move the straw to one end of the string and let go of the balloon.
7. Watch your rocket fly!
8. Repeat steps 3–7 two more times, but change the length of the straw each time to see if this has any effect on the distance your rocket travels. Try to add the same amount of air to the balloon each time so you are only changing one variable: the length of the straw.
9. Record your observations in the data table below.

	Length of Straw (in.)	Distance Rocket Traveled (in.)
Trial 1		
Trial 2		
Trial 3		

10. Which length of straw allowed for the farthest rocket launch? Why do you think this length provided the best launch distance? _____

_____

_____

_____

Social Studies Activity

BONUS

Which Colony Am I?

Each of the Thirteen Colonies had different characteristics that made them unique. Using a textbook, encyclopedia, or other reference, conduct research and write which colony each clue describes.

Connecticut   Delaware   Georgia   Maryland   Massachusetts
New Hampshire   New Jersey   New York   North Carolina   Pennsylvania
Rhode Island   South Carolina   Virginia

1. _____ This colony was founded by Lords Proprietors in 1663 as part of a larger colony. Its economy was based on enslaved labor, and its major city was Charleston.
2. _____ This New England territory became a royal colony in 1679. It was the most northern of the Thirteen Colonies, with an economy based on fishing, shipbuilding, and timber.
3. _____ This colony was the first of the Thirteen Colonies to be established, starting with a settlement at Jamestown.
4. _____ This colony was first settled by the Swedes, centered in Fort Christina, before being taken over by the Dutch and later the English.
5. _____ This New England colony was formed under the leadership of Thomas Hooker. Its economy was centered on shipbuilding, manufacturing, and rum exports.
6. _____ Founded in 1732 by James Oglethorpe, this colony was originally meant for those who were in prison for debt and as a place where slavery was not to be practiced.
7. _____ This colony was first founded by a group of Separatists at Plymouth in 1630.
8. _____ This colony was founded in 1682 and was originally heavily settled by Quakers.
9. _____ The Dutch founded this colony in 1614. Its original name was New Netherland.
10. _____ This colony was founded by Roger Williams in 1636 and promoted religious freedom.
11. _____ This colony was separated from a larger colony. Its economy was based on the production of rice and other agricultural products by enslaved labor.
12. _____ This Middle Colony was given over to Sir George Carteret and Lord John Berkley after it was taken by the English from the Dutch.
13. _____ This colony was founded by Lord Baltimore in 1632 as a haven for English Catholics.

BONUS

Social Studies Activity

Translating the Bill of Rights (continued)

The first ten amendments to the U.S. Constitution are called the Bill of Rights. These amendments provide important protections to American citizens and help to support a democratic society. Sometimes these amendments are hard to understand, however, because of the way they were written centuries ago. In this activity, read the amendments of the Bill of Rights. Then, in the space provided, summarize the meaning of the amendment in plain language.

1. **Eighth Amendment**

    Excessive bail shall not be required, nor excessive fines imposed, nor cruel and unusual punishments inflicted.

    _____
    _____
    _____

2. **Ninth Amendment**

    The enumeration in the Constitution, of certain rights, shall not be construed to deny or disparage others retained by the people.

    _____
    _____
    _____

3. **Tenth Amendment**

    The powers not delegated to the United States by the Constitution, nor prohibited by it to the States, are reserved to the States respectively, or to the people.

    _____
    _____
    _____

> **CHARACTER CHECK:** What is something you can do to show respect for yourself?

© Carson Dellosa Education

Social Studies Activity

BONUS

Geographic Features of the United States

The United States has many important geographic features. Study the map below. Then, mark off the listed physical feature with the letter shown on the map.

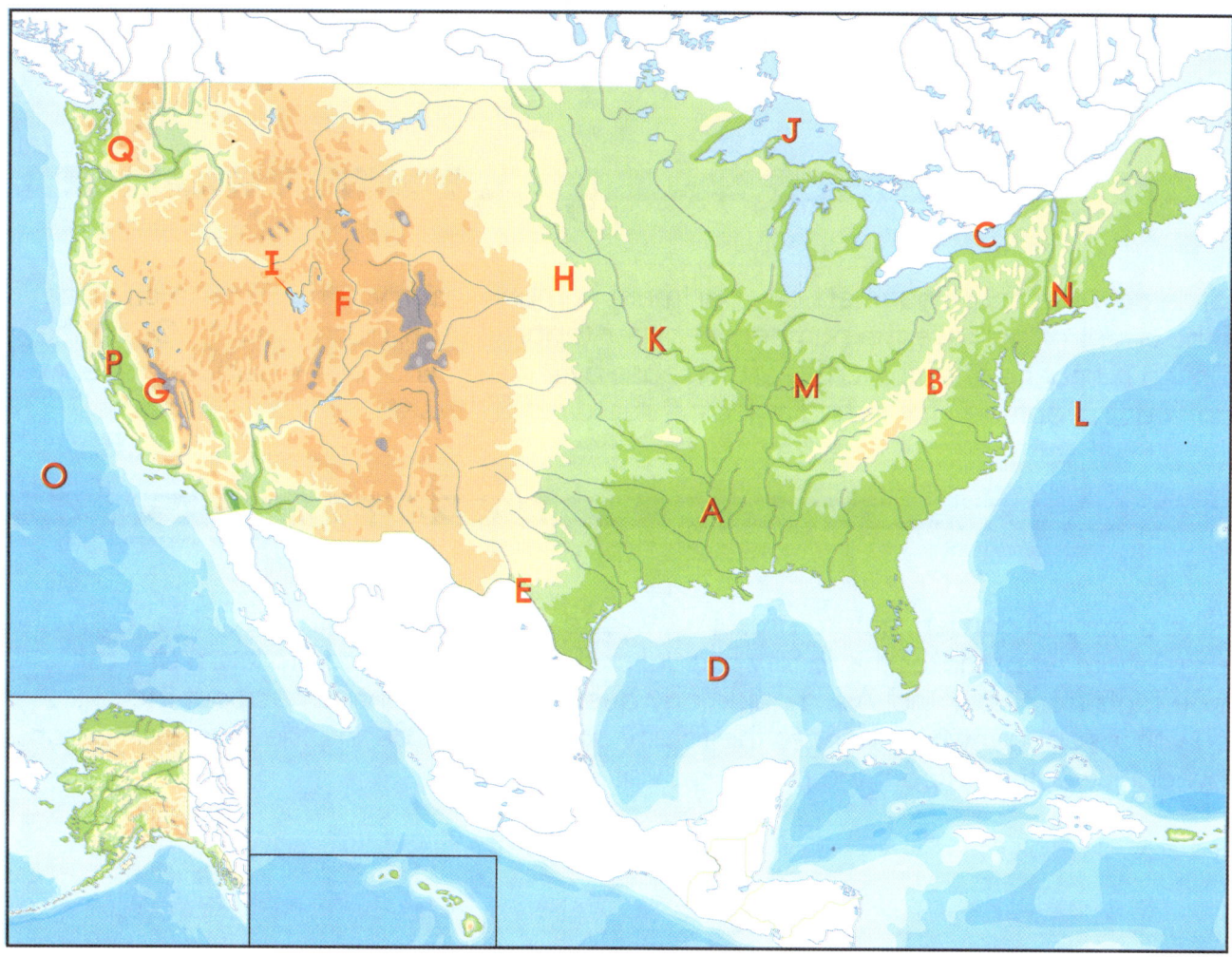

1. _____ Hudson River
2. _____ Missouri River
3. _____ Appalachian Mountains
4. _____ Great Salt Lake
5. _____ Gulf of Mexico
6. _____ Lake Ontario
7. _____ Rocky Mountains
8. _____ Pacific Ocean
9. _____ Lake Superior
10. _____ Great Plains
11. _____ Ohio River
12. _____ Mississippi River
13. _____ Central Valley
14. _____ Sierra Nevada
15. _____ Cascade Range
16. _____ Rio Grande
17. _____ Atlantic Ocean

Outdoor Extension Activities

BONUS

Take It Outside!

Plant something—either a flower, fruit, or vegetable—from seed outdoors. Watch the life cycle of the plant over the summer as it grows. Record observations about how the life cycle of the plant changes. Identify the parts of the plant: roots, stem, bud, flower, and fruit. Bean and sunflower plants are great for this, as they grow quickly and can show more significant change from day to day.

Notice how the house numbers or apartment numbers near you change on one side of the street or hall. Are the numbers in order (apartment 3, apartment 4)? Or do they follow a number pattern, such as an increase by 2 or 4? What other number patterns can you find outside? Try to find at least three different types of numeric patterns.

Visit a botanical garden, nature preserve, wildlife center, or any other outdoor center. Learn about what makes this facility special and challenge yourself to learn at least three facts from your trip. Ask a guide any questions you might have about the place you visit. Ask about what changes the facility goes through during the different seasons. How does weather impact the place you visited?

Section I

Day 1/Page 3: 1. function; 2. function; 3. not a function; 4. not a function; 5. function; 6. function; 7. gerund; 8. participle; 9. infinitive; 10. participle; 11. participle; 12. infinitive; 13. gerund; 14. ab**hor**: regard with disgust and hatred; 15. **bi**sect: divide into two parts; 16. con**jec**ture: an opinion or conclusion formed on the basis of incomplete information; 17. waxing gibbous; 18. full moon; 19. third quarter; 20. waning crescent; 21. new moon; 22. first quarter

Day 2/Page 5:

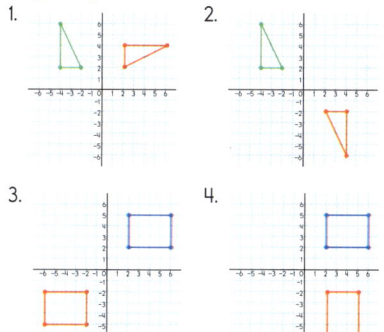

5. The orchardist grows pears, cherries, and apples.; 6. Time seemed to stand still as Layla's mom opened the envelope, frowning at the report.; 7. The Oz family bought towels, shovels, and chairs at the shop; they carried it all as they ran toward the sandy beach.; 8. The pile of laundry, never seeming to diminish, was constantly taunting Sam.; 9. Fall brought cooler temperatures, crunching leaves beneath their feet, and the aroma of pumpkin spice.; 10. C; 11. A; 12. C; 13. C; 14. B; 15. A; 16. The author's purpose is to inform and provide information.

Day 3/Page 7: 1. 0.15; 2. $\frac{m}{1} = \frac{36\div}{6}$, 6.125; 3. $\frac{f}{1} = \frac{16\div}{5}$, 3.3; 4. daunting; 5. immunity; 6. summons; 7. fickle; 8. restriction; 9. ceremonial; 10. A; 11. C

Day 4/Page 9: 1. $x = -7$; 2. $y = 4$; 3. $a = 10$; 4. $x = -24$; 5. $q = \frac{1}{2}$; 6. $y = 43$; 7. $s = 72$; 8. $a = 9$; 9. adequate; 10. blemish; 11. lapse; 12. haphazard; 13. debris; 14. boon; 15. A; 16. B; 17. B; 18. A; 19. B; 20. A; Student responses will vary.

Day 5/Page 11: 1. Reflection over the y-axis; 2. $A'(5, 1)$; 3. $B'(2, -4)$; 4. $\frac{1}{3}$; 5. $\frac{1}{4}$; 6. $1\frac{1}{2}$; 7. root word: lecture, suffix: -er; 8. root word: judge, prefix: mis-; 9. root word: fabricate, prefix: pre-, suffix: -ed; 10. root word: honor, prefix: dis-; 11. root word: mortal, prefix: im, suffix: -ity

Day 6/Page 13:

1.

	Carrots	No Carrots	Total
Potatoes	38	7	45
No Potatoes	34	47	81
Total	72	54	126

2.

	Lunch	No Lunch	Total
Regular Pass	132	148	280
Premium Pass	52	18	70
Total	184	166	350

3. Last night's math homework frustrated me.; 4. The results of the experiment surprised the scientists.; 5. Jack's neighbor Sam broke the window.; 6. B; 7. C; 8. Turtles use the subtle shifts in the magnetic field of the Earth's core to guide them on their migratory path.

Day 7/Page 15: 1. B': (1, −4), C': (3, 0), D': (0, 2);

2.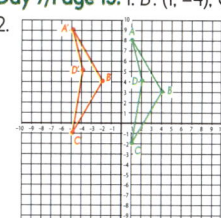

Pre-image coordinates: A: (1, 8), B: (4, 3), C: (1, −2), D: (2, 4). Image coordinates: A': (−5, 9), B': (−2, 4), C': (−5, −1), D': (−4, 5);

3. I; 4. IN; 5. IM; 6. C; 7. IN; 8. IM; 9. I; 10. IN; 11. C; 12. B; 13. A; 14. C; 15. B; 16. D; 17. biter; 18. hiker; 19. rides (17–19. Other answers may be possible.)

Day 8/Page 17: 1. dependent; 2. $\frac{1}{10}$; 3. $3\frac{1}{13}$; 4. Take turns going down the slide and then eat your snack.; 5. As the school bus turned the corner, the riders heard a clunking sound.; 6. She went to the grocery store and bought some snacks.; 7. Take a picture and then make the memory last.; 8. to pass with flying colors: to pass a test easily or with a high score; 9. to add fuel to the fire: to make an existing problem worse; 10. up in the air: undecided; 11. fish out of water: to not belong or fit in somewhere; 12. lion's share: the biggest portion; 13. down to the wire: waiting until the last minute; 14. crocodile tears: false tears; 15. on the same page: to feel the same way

Day 9/Page 19: 1. $\frac{21}{80}$; 2. $\frac{1}{9}$; 3. $\frac{1}{4}$; 4. $\frac{1}{153}$; 5. In 1775, the continental congress appointed the first postmaster general. The person was a historical figure who was familiar to most people: benjamin franklin. Franklin helped to organize and develop the united states postal service, which is still in operation today, more than 200 years later. The first postage stamps were issued in 1847. In 1860, as the united states was expanding west, the pony express was born. Over time, the U.S. postal service has continued to adapt, and letter carriers still work to deliver mail around the world today.; 6. B; 7. C; 8. They teach us much about how ordinary people lived in the past.

Day 10/Page 21: 1. These events are disjoint because it is impossible to roll a 1 and an even number at the same time, since 1 is not even.;

2.

These events are disjoint because Event A describes only the number 6, which is not an odd number. These events cannot occur at the same time.; 3.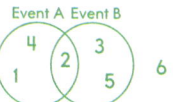

These events are overlapping because the number 2 belongs to Event A and is also a prime number, which describes Event B.; 4. After the winter storm, it was difficult to walk up the slippery, steep driveway.; 5. While I was finishing my breakfast, the school bus arrived.; 6. I was born in Rochester, New York, on January 28, 2006.; 7. Before she leaves for baseball, Leila packs her bag with a water bottle, her baseball glove, her helmet, and her bat.; 8. Ani was exhausted from a long day of school and babysitting, but he had to finish his homework before he could go to sleep.; 9. Dylan, please take your shoes off before coming inside.; 10. *Divergent*, a book by Veronica Roth, takes place in the future.; 11. integrate; 12. novice; 13. simulate; 14. bisect; 15. evoke; 16. authority; Student drawings will vary.

Day 11/Page 23: 1. greater than; 2. greater than; 3. you, P; 4. anyone, I; 5. that, D; 6. Nobody, I; 7. those, D; 8. we, P; 9. everyone, I; 10. this, D; 11. us, P; 12. most, I; 13. a; 14. B; 15. C; 16. A; 17. A; 18. B; 19. D; 20. A; 21. Antarctica and Australia

Day 12/Page 25: 1. 6,380; 2. 97.50; 3. 30; 4. For my last birthday, my parents gave me a bicycle.; 5. AV; 6. AV; 7. The magician's tricks amazed the audience.; 8. Every Thanksgiving, the guests gobble up Juan's pecan pie.; 9. drama; 10. poetry; 11. fable; 12. autobiography; 13. myth; 14. historical fiction; Students' writing will vary.

Day 13/Page 27: 1. $h = 8$; 2. $w = 5$; 3. $c = -4$; 4. $r = \frac{8}{9}$; 5. $t = -43$; 6. $q = -5$; 7. $z = 15$; 8. $s = 16$; 9. 1) Translate right 2 units and up 3 units. 2) Reflect across the y-axis. (Answers may vary.); 10. 1) Rotate 180° about the origin. 2) Translate up 3 units. (Answers may vary.); 11. C; 12. B; 13. July 2025, in the Armstrongs' backyard

Day 14/Page 29: 1. $10ab - 2a$; 2. $16x + 5y$; 3. $4n^2 + n$; 4. $6a^2$; 5. $3b^2 + 9c^2$; 6. $-x^2 + 4x - 5y$; 7. us, O; 8. she, N; 9. I, N; 10. them, O; 11. he, N; 12. he, N; 13. us, O; 14. me, O; 15. they, N; 16. her, O; 17. B; 18. Balto was the lead dog of the last dogsled team to arrive and would have been given more attention in the news.; Student responses will vary.

Day 15/Page 31: 1. $x = 7$; 2. $x = 3$; 3. $x = -2$; 4. $x = 4$; 5. $x = -1$; 6. $x = 7$; 7. I; 8. R; 9. R; 10. R; 11. R; 12. I; 13. R; 14. R; 15. I; 16. R; The United States has two coasts on opposite sides of the country—one along the Atlantic Ocean and one along the Pacific Ocean. These coasts are aptly named the East Coast and the West Coast. The West Coast is made up of California, Oregon, and Washington, while the East Coast is made up of 14 states that border the Atlantic. The West Coast experiences a relatively mild climate year round. Most of the states along the East Coast experience all four seasons. Other than differences in physical location, there are differences in how people in these regions behave. People on the East Coast are thought of as more uptight and fast paced, while people on the West Coast are more liberal and casual. There are differences in types of food eaten on both coasts, too. West Coast diners favor organic and healthier options, whereas East Coast diners favor fast food and carb-laden options. Because both coasts are near an ocean, they are filled with people who enjoy the coastal regions for recreation and plentiful seafood. Regardless of your coastal preference, we can agree that anyone who lives near the beach is lucky.

Day 16/Page 33: 1. $136.00; 2. 31 mm or 3.1 cm; 3. 11 lb.; Answers will vary but may include the following: 4. hideous; 5. brave; 6. giving; 7. weak; 8. firm; 9. dislike; 10. exact; 11. spoil; 12. exile; 13. purity; 14. C; 15. B; 16. The genome sequence helps scientists understand genetic diseases and learn ways to treat these diseases.

Day 17/Page 35: 1. $9\frac{73}{100}$; 2. $\frac{431}{500}$; 3. $\frac{47}{99}$; 4. $7\frac{3}{20}$; 5. $5\frac{1}{5}$; 6. $\frac{83}{90}$; 7. $3\frac{4}{9}$; 8. $13\frac{1}{10}$; 9. Q; 10. P; 11. U; 12. P; 13. Q; 14. plot; 15. symbol; 16. simile; 17. protagonist; 18. personification; 19. foreshadowing; 20. inference; 21. characterization; 22. conflict; 23. setting; 24. labor; 25. scarcity; 26. resources; 27. demand; 28. monopoly; 29. supply; 30. consumer; 31. recession; 32. capitalism; 33. capital

Day 18/Page 37: 1. $x > 3$; 2. $x > 2$; 3. $x \geq -3$; 4. $x < -4$; 5. $x \geq 48$; 6. $x \leq 2$; anonymously; separate; dissatisfied; received; accommodate; outrageously; successful; 7. 180 degrees; 8. 90 degrees; 9. 270 degrees; Electromagnetic Spectrum answers: G; H; D; F; B; J; K; I; L

Day 19/Page 39: 1. 3^5; 2. 6^3; 3. 2^{-6}; 4. 7^6; 5. 8^4; 6. 2^{-16}; 7. 5^2; 8. 3^{20}; Pronoun activity answers: her; his; They; them; their; she; she; their; they; 9. B; 10. B; 11. Student answers will vary.

Day 20/Page 41: 1. 20.4; 2. 2,270; 3. 6.50; 4. its, P; 5. You're, C; 6. their, P; 7. your, P; 8. It's, C; 9. They're, C; 10. F; 11. T; 12. T; 13. F; 14. T; 15. T; 16. F; Student responses will vary.

Bonus Page 47: 1. Atlanta; 2. Toronto; 3. Madrid; 4. Beijing; 5. Sydney; 6. Los Angeles; 7. Manila; 8. Cape Town; 9. 35°S 58°W; 10. 30°N 31°E; 11. 48°N 107°E; 12. 42°N 88°W; 13. 41°S 175°E; 14. 60°N 30°E; 15. 9°N 39°E; 16. 23°N 82°W

Section II

Day 1/Page 51: 1. $2 < x < 9$; 2. $c \leq 5$; 3. $5 \leq d \leq 12$; 4. $t \geq 1$; 5. $g < -20$ or $g > -7$; 6. $3 < z < 10$; 7. Julia is playing volleyball again; she is learning many new skills.; 8. The students refused to do their homework; they said it was too difficult.; 9. It was rush hour; the city streets were filled with people hurrying to catch their trains home.; 10. Ryan practices the violin for three hours each day; he is a focused and talented musician.; 11. Walking is a great form of exercise; it strengthens your muscles and improves your circulation.; 12–13. Answers will vary. 14. cluttered/tidied up; 15. small/drastic; 16. zeal/disinterest; 17. concise/long; 18. chloroplast; 19. vacuole; 20. cell wall; 21. nucleus; 22. Golgi body; 23. cytoplasm; 24. mitochondria; 25. ribosome

Day 2/Page 53: 1. $t = \frac{d}{s}$; 2. $m = \frac{F}{a}$; 3. $v = at + u$; 4. $p = \pm\sqrt{\frac{q-1}{2}}$; 5. $y = \frac{C-Ax}{B}$; 6. $a = \pm\sqrt{c^2 - b^2}$; 7. $m = \frac{E}{c^2}$; 8. $b = \frac{dc - 2a}{2}$ or $b = \frac{dc}{2} + a$; 9–14. Sample responses given. 9. Renee ate a piece of juicy watermelon at the picnic.; 10. The large dinner table was big enough for all five guests.; 11. Dante's brother rolled around in the wet grass.; 12. When the quick rabbit heard us coming, it hopped back into the woods.; 13. I looked out my window and saw that the ground was covered in fresh snow.; 14. Mia wore a red dress to the graduation ceremony. 15. C; 16. B; 17. C

Day 3/Page 55: 1. (0, 2); 2. (0, −1); 3. (0, −6); 4. (0, −3); 5. (0, 2); 6. (0, −10); 7. empty; 8. a youthful person; 9. across or through; 10. light; 11. water; 12. of both kinds; 13. foot; 14. two; 15. under; 16. outside normal events; 17–21. Letters in green should be circled. 17. abate, verb, to become less intense or widespread; 18. lament, verb, to express grief or sorrow; 19. deliberate, adjective, carefully weighed or considered; 20. ornate, adjective, decorated with complicated patterns or shapes; 21. pilfer, verb, to steal especially in small quantities; 22. $m = 2$; 23. $m = -\frac{1}{3}$; 24. $m = \frac{5}{4}$

Day 4/Page 57: Written responses will vary.; 1. stayed; 2. closed; 3. will start; 4. was delivered; 5. has been playing; 6. fell; 7. is; 8. improve 9. A; 10. A; 11. B; 12. D; 13. C; 14. B; 15. B; 16. B

Day 5/Page 59: 1. 3; 2. 1; 3. -4; 4. -3; 5. 4; 6. -1; 7. 1; 8. 0; I recently visited the Metropolitan Museum of Art in New York City. While I expected the museum to be filled with works of art like paintings and sculptures, I did not expect it to contain so many historical artifacts. The museum's Egyptian wing, for example, has an amazing collection of mummies. I also saw jewelry and household objects like bowls and perfume bottles that the ancient Egyptians used. The exhibit even contained an actual Egyptian temple, the Temple of Dendur, which was built over two thousand years ago. Another fascinating glimpse into the past was the arms and armor exhibit. I saw suits of armor worn by people (and horses!) throughout history and around the world, and the museum even had a suit of armor worn by King Henry the VIII of England. For me, the museum really made history come alive! 9. C; 10. B; 11. B and D; 12. Taking flight requires lift. Because Mars has a very low level of atmospheric gases, it is hard to create this force of lift.

Day 6/Page 61: 1. linear function; 2. linear function; 3. nonlinear function; 4. linear function; 5. nonlinear function; 6. linear function; 7. a beacon, M; 8. is a river that flows in only one direction, M; 9. like a warm hug around me, S; 10. a whisper, M; 11. as soft as velvet, S; 12. like a seed planted in my mind, S; 13. automate, -ion; 14. harmony, -ize; 15. disrepute, -able; 16. compare, -ative; 17. invigorate, -ing; 18. grieve, -ance; 19. displace, -ment; 20. dispense, -able; 21. defense, -ive; 22. custody, -ian; Student answers will vary.

Day 7/Page 63: 1. 31%; 2. $8.28; 3. 933 birds; 4. $14.60; 5. $477.54; 6. 4.8 oz; 7. $2,166.67; 8. 65%; 9. 0.12; 10. 0.35; 11. 0.40; Aisha: frog; Jake: cat; Jayden: snake; Kym: bird; Tierra: rabbit

Day 8/Page 65: 1. 10, 5; 2. 5, 9; 3. 4, 8; 4–5. Sample answers given. 4. Alex, an excellent public speaker, won first place at the debate competition.; 5. Because Alex is an excellent public speaker, he won first place at the debate competition. 6. D.; 7. It is marked by religious activities and celebrations.

Day 9/Page 67: 1. 3; 2. 20; 3. 11; 4. 7; 5. 5; 6. 1; 7. I; 8. IN; 9. C; 10. I; 11. IN; 12. IM; 13. C; 14. IN; 15. I; 16. IM; 17. A; 18. B; 19. B; 20. A; 21. A; 22. B; 23. A; 24. B; 25-26. Student answers will vary.

Day 10/Page 69: 1. $y = 0.2x - 4$; 2. $y = -5x + 38$; 3. $y = 6x - 7$; 4. $y = \frac{3}{4}x - 22$; 5. $y + 8 = -3(x - 11)$; 6. $y - 9 = -\frac{7}{10}(x + 3)$; 7. collecting; 8. skiing; 9. Baking; 10. Practicing; 11. Listening; 12. gardening; 13. dreaming; 14. moving; 15. planning; 16. asking; 17. B; 18. D; 19. B; Types of Rocks: C, D, E, A, I, J, F, B, G, H

Day 11/Page 71: 1. 2.8 hot dogs per minute, 2.96 hot dogs per minute, fewer; 2. 0.16 miles per minute or 9.6 miles per hour, 0.17 miles per minute or 10 miles per hour, slower; 3. $3.25 per mile, $4 per mile, less.; 4. A or F; 5. E; 6. C; 7. G; 8. B; 9. D; 10. F; 11. D; 12. B; 13. Student answers will vary.

Day 12/Page 73: 1. A': (−3, −2), B': (0,0), C': (−4, −5), D': (−2, −5); 2. A': (−4, 4), B': (−9, −8), C': (−4, −4), D': (−9, 2); 3. A': (1, −6), B': (6, −6), C': (6, 0), D': (−2, 0); 4. A': (−9, −9), B': (−7, 12), C': (3, −8), D': (5, −4); 5. whether/or; 6. neither/nor; 7. both/and (or not only/but also); 8. not only/but also; 9. Either/or; 10. B; 11. by diverting the supply of water to the lake

Day 13/Page 75: 1. 5 and 6; 2. 7 and 8; 3. 9 and 10; 4. 4, $\sqrt{17}$, 5, $\sqrt{29}$; 5. 3, $\sqrt{19}$, 7, $\sqrt{51}$; 6. 4, $\sqrt{24}$, 5, $\sqrt{39}$; 7. After school I will go to orchestra rehearsal, and then I will walk home.; 8. The top row of books was very dusty.; 9. The number of job applicants is much higher than Mr. Pappas expected.; 10. When Leo visited Boston, he went to see the site of the first battle of the Revolutionary War. OR When Leo visits Boston, he goes to see the site of the first battle of the Revolutionary War. Student writing will vary.

Day 14/Page 77: 1. 2, 35; 2. 14, −11; 3. 0.5, 0.75; 4. 12, 16; 5. 21, 118; 6. 4.3, 5.7; 7. Before we played football, the field needed to be cleaned.; 8. After I practiced my solo for a week, my music teacher said I would be ready for the concert.; 9. The car's lights were on as it drove down the dark street.; 10. We saw both dolphins and whales jumping out of the waves when we went sailing.; 11. When I finished my watercolor painting, my art teacher said I was ready for oil painting next. 12. A; 13. Answers will vary. The theme is appreciating each day.; 14. Answers will vary.

Day 15/Page 79: 1. solution, not a solution, solution; 2. not a solution, not a solution, solution; 3.

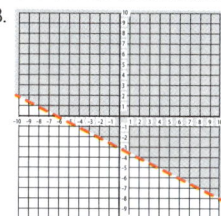

4.

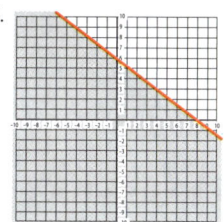

5. pool, <u>swimming</u>; 6. painting, <u>lost</u>; 7. apples, <u>dried</u>; 8. wheel, <u>spinning</u>; 9. puppy, <u>lost</u>; 10. narrative; 11. expository; 12. narrative; 13. descriptive; 14. persuasive; 15. expository; 16. wolf; 17. zebra; 18. anemone; 19. desert tortoise

Day 16/Page 81: 1. (10, 2); 2. (13, 4); 3. (9, 3); 4. hate; 5. nameless; 6. bounced; 7. unlivable; 8. impossible to deny; 9. stubborn; 10. C; 11. There are likely fewer lobsters because they used to just wash up on the shore, but they do not anymore.; 12. Student answers will vary.; 13. H; 14. D; 15. B; 16. A; 17. F; 18. C; 19. E; 20. G

Day 17/Page 83: 1. Possible answer: Dilation of scale factor 2 through the origin and a reflection over the y-axis.; 2. Possible answer: Rotation by 90° clockwise about the origin and a dilation of scale factor $\frac{1}{3}$ through the origin.; 3. Circle *cities*, underline *are*, and draw arrows to *Tokyo* and *Delhi*.; 4. Circle *emperor*, underline *was*, and draw an arrow to *Qin Shi Huang*.; 5. Circle *Mariana Trench*, underline *is*, and draw an arrow to *point*.; 6. Circle *mountains*, underline *are*, draw an arrow to *Alps*.; 7. Circle *queen*, underline *has been*, and draw an arrow to *Queen Elizabeth II*.; 8. Circle *capital*, underline *became*, and draw an arrow to *Washington, D.C.* 9. A; 10. C; 11. There was a bill, which is a primary source, from the time. The bill indicates that Hopkinson made it.

Day 18/Page 85: 1. $y = 6x − 3$; 2. $y = −45x + 6$; 3. $y = −32x − 2$; 4. $y = 98x + 12$; 5. $y = x + 1$; 6. $y = −16x − 34$; 7. brought, will bring; 8. sang, will sing; 9. sought, will seek; 10. tore, will tear; 11. sneezed, will sneeze; 12. swam, will swim; 13. caught, will catch; 14. began, will begin; 15. bought, will buy; 16. taught, will teach; 17. formal; 18. informal; 19. formal; 20. formal; 21. informal; 22. formal; 23. Law #2; 24. Law #1; 25. Law #3; 26. Law #3; 27. Law #2; 28. Law #1

Day 19/Page 87: 1. dilate with scale factor 2 about the origin; 2. Sample answer: rotate 180° about the origin, and dilate by scale factor $\frac{1}{2}$ about the origin; 3. Sample answer: dilate with scale factor $\frac{1}{3}$ about the origin, and translate left 5 units and down 2 units; 4. 12; 5. 11; 6. 77.5; 7. 58; 8. wind howled fiercely; 9. plant thirstily drank; 10. leaves danced, wind gently pushed; 11. aroma whispered my name; 12. Time refused to move; 13. truck was tired and thirsty; 14. sun peeked out shyly; 15. garbage disposal roared its appreciation; Student answers will vary.

Day 20/Page 89: 1. $5x + 2$; 2. $−3a + 7$; 3. $7r + 8$; 4. $9b − 7$; 5. $8z + 10$; 6. $−2c + 2$; 7. $26z + 2$; 8. $16c − 19$; 9. adjective; 10. conjunction; 11. noun; 12. noun; 13. adjective; 14. verb; 15. D; 16. Modern computers are smaller than older computers and more powerful.; 17. Computers are likely to continue to get smaller and more powerful.

Bonus Page 92: Student answers will vary. The original cabbage juice should be purple, with acids like vinegar and citrus juice turning redder, and bases like soap turning more blue or green. Some examples of pHs are listed below:
- lemon or lime juice: 2
- white vinegar: 2 to 3
- orange juice: 4
- milk: (neutral) 6 to 7
- baking soda: 8
- hand soap: 9 to 10
- laundry detergent: 10

Bonus Page 93: 1. Vasco da Gama; 2. Jacques Cartier; 3. Christopher Columbus; 4. John Cabot; 5. Ferdinand Magellan; 6. Hernando de Soto; 7. Henry Hudson; 8. Amerigo Vespucci; 9. Juan Ponce de Leon; 10. Vasco Nunez de Balboa

Bonus Page 94: Student answers may vary. 1. guarantees U.S. citizens specific rights, including not having to testify against yourself if accused of a crime, and the "right to remain silent"; 2. provides protections to accused persons, right to speedy public trial, impartial jury, accused may provide own witnesses; 3. provides the right to trial by jury in federal civil cases

Bonus Page 95: 1. 1963; 2. 1954; 3. 1961; 4. 1965; 5. 1955; 6. 1948; 7. 1968; 8. 1957

Section III

Day 1/Page 99: 1. 17; 2. 16; 3. 26.4; 4. 7.6; 5. 6.2; 6. 15.7; 7. F; 8. A; 9. D; 10. E; 11. C; 12. B; 13. H; 14. I; 15. J; 16. G; 17. brazen; 18. contours; 19. flank; 20. feudal; 21. intangible; 22. 0.000042; 23. 156,000; 24. 2,500,000; 25. 64.3; 26. 782,400,000; 27. 29,480,000; 28. −1,935

Day 2/Page 101: 1. $AC = 5.7$; 2. $FG = 9.0$; 3. $AC = 13$; 4. $FE = 5.2$; 5. $AF = 11.3$; 6. $BG = 17$, $AG = 19.2$; 7. B; 8. C; 9. pilfer; 10. malicious; 11. smite; 12. luminous; 13. formidable; Student answers will vary.

Day 3/Page 103: 1. 1,768; 2. 6,123; 3. 5,150; 4. 74,217; 5. 53,400; 6. 50,874; 7. 2,180; 8. 3,125; 9. cooking, cook; 10. washing, wash; 11. arriving, arrive; 12. sipping, sip; 13. eating, eat; 14. walking, walk; 15. surfing, surf; 16. D; 17. C; 18. A; 19. B; 20. One cup of sugar is used in step 2, and 1 cup of sugar is used in step 3.

Day 4/Page 105: 1. (−2, −8); 2. (4, 13); 3. (−7, 5); 4. (3, −3); 5. (10, 1); 6. (213, 13); 7. to inform readers about bee hives and the roles that different bees play in the hive; 8. to entertain readers with a fictional story about a character named Ronan; 9. to persuade or convince readers that getting a dog is beneficial to families; 10. D; 11. C; 12. F; 13. A; 14. H; 15. G; 16. E; 17. I; 18. J; 19. B

Day 5/Page 107: 1. 22 years old; 2. 14 yellow shirts; 3. $2.00; 4. 5 lb; 5–8. Sample interjections given. 5. Wow!; 6. Phew!; 7. Look!; 8. Oops; Answers may vary: my mind was racing; the baseball field is my sanctuary; my stomach dropped like an out-of-control elevator; glared at me like a tiger eyeing its prey; my nerves would vanish like dust in the air; my glove kept my secret; his long, silver bat taunting me; I have done this a million times; smack; the ball flew by Jonah; after what feels like an eternity.; 9. E; 10. C; 11. D; 12. A; 13. B; 14. Producers get their energy from the sun through the process of photosynthesis.

Day 6/Page 109: 1. 224 m; 2. 5.7 in.; 3. 6.5 cm; The Nazca Lines are a **mysterious** collection of giant figures drawn on a **desert** plain about 250 miles **south** of Lima, Peru. The drawings, which are over 2,000 years old, **include** straight **lines**, geometric shapes, and giant animals, such as a spider, a monkey, and a duck. The figures are so large that they can only be seen from the air. Archeologists today **wonder** why they were **made**. **Were** they part of a **ceremony** asking the gods for rain? Were they an astronomical calendar? We will probably never solve the **mystery** of the Nazca Lines; 4. B;

5. He might be happy at its popularity but upset at how its overuse endangers it.; 6. The trail connects across different states, making it national in nature.

Day 7/Page 111: 1. one; 2. none; 3. one; 4. infinite; 5. one; 6. infinite; 7. B; 8. D; 9. A; 10. E; 11. C; 12. B; 13. The size of the massive stones of the monument would have impressed others.; 14. They are both unfounded theories.

Day 8/Page 113: 1. $(x-5)(x+2)$; 2. $(y+7)(y+8)$; 3. $(z-3)(z-3)$; 4. $(a+\frac{1}{2})(a+\frac{2}{3})$; 5. $(2b-9)(5b+11)$; 6. $(8c-6)(-10c-4)$; 7. $(9m+1)(9m+1)$; 8. $(-\frac{1}{2}n+12)(n-1)$; 9. **mor**, adjective, lacking physical form or shape; 10. **the**, adjective, extremely light or delicate; 11. **sa**, adjective, impossible to satisfy; 12. **gev**, noun, long life; 13. **clude**, verb, to make impossible; 14. **sub**, noun, deception used to achieve an end; 15. **zeal**, adjective, filled with enthusiasm

16. maladjustment	mal	adjust	ment
17. dissimilar	dis	similar	
18. characterize		character	ize
19. reformatory	re	form	atory
20. commentary		comment	ary

Day 9/Page 115: 1. 5.39; 2. 8.94; 3. 4.47; 4. PV; 5. Jamie read thirty pages of the history textbook last night.; 6. PV; 7. PV; 8. My mother painted the ceiling and the walls.; 9. PV; 10. A; 11. C; 12. B; Chemical: combining vinegar and milk to make buttermilk, baking a cake, steeping tea leaves, lighting a campfire, roasting a marshmallow; Physical: cracking an egg, mixing cake batter, boiling water, cooling tea with ice, sandwiching chocolate and marshmallow between graham crackers

Day 10/Page 117: 1. 62.8 cm³; 2. 162.5 ft³; 3. 12.4 in.³; 4. 147.2 cm³; 5. which; 6. who; 7. who; 8. that; 9. whom; 10. that; 11. D; 12. A; 13. E; 14. B; 15. C; 16. textbook; 17. lemonade or water; 18. water; 19. helium gas; 20. pencil; 21. oxygen gas

Day 11/Page 119: 1. 50.3 cm³; 2. 1866.1 ft³; 3. 11.8 in.³; 4. 66.9 m³; 5. 15 in.; 6. 6 vases; Student answers will vary.; 7. C; 8. D; 9. D; 10. Student answers will vary.

Day 12/Page 121: 1. 2,144.66 ft³; 2. 137.26 m³; 3. 904.78 cm³; 4. 268.08 in.³; 5. 523.60 μm³; 6. 113.10 in.³; 7. S: Adriana, DO: quilts; 8. S: mother, DO: puzzle; 9. S: Carson, DO: "Moonlight Sonata"; 10. S: detective, DO: footprint; 11. S: Monique, DO: "Hansel and Gretel"; 12. S: I, DO: Tyler; 13. S: chef, DO: parsley; 14. S: We, DO: *The Lion King*; 15. C; 16. A; 17. Males huddle together for warmth, parents have brood pouches to keep the egg warm, ability to fast for long periods of time while incubating eggs, deep dives to search for food

Day 13/Page 123: 1. (2, −2); 2. (−3, −13); 3. $(\frac{3}{4}, \frac{39}{8})$; 4. (4, 6); 5. $x = 2$; 6. $x = -\frac{3}{2}$; 7. chronological; 8. sequence; 9. compare/contrast; 10. descriptive; Renewable: biomass, geothermal, hydropower, wind, solar; Non-renewable: coal, natural gas, nuclear, petroleum; Wood/timber can arguably belong in either category. It can be renewable if grown rapidly and cut down slowly, or non-renewable if used at a higher rate than it is produced.

Day 14/Page 125: 1. positive correlation; 2. no correlation; 3. no correlation; 4. negative correlation; 5. negative correlation; 6. positive correlation; 7. Logos because the writer uses a statistic to explain the importance of reading.; 8. Ethos because the writer appeals to the emotions of the audience by talking about cozying up with a young child and sharing a story, and about how young children love to spend time with their families.; 9. Ethos because the writer establishes her credibility by explaining that she has twenty-five years of teaching experience.

Day 15/Page 127: 1. increasing; 2. decreasing; 3. decreasing; 4. increasing; 5. increasing; 6. decreasing; 7. increasing; 8. increasing; 9. increasing; 10. increasing; 11. B; 12. D; 13. B; 14. C; 15. A; 16. D; 17. D; 18. C; 19. President Barack Obama

Day 16/Page 129: 1. $\frac{1}{4}$; 2. about 3:2; 3. Answers will vary.; 4. O; 5. A; 6. O; 7. A; 8. O; 9. O; 10. A; 11. C; 12. (Answers may vary.) Daedalus is thoughtful and makes plans, while Icarus acts according to how he feels and does not consider the results.; Punnett square top row: Rr, rr; bottom row: Rr, rr; 13. Rr and rr; 14. Round or wrinkled peas; 15. 50% round; 16. 50% wrinkled

Day 17/Page 131: 1. 25.12; 2. 904.32; 3. 8,138.88; Student answers will vary.; (Answers will vary.) Safety is important as individuals are learning to drive a vehicle. Your seat belt should be put on as soon as you sit in the vehicle. Mirrors need to be checked and modified before starting the vehicle. It is important to always check around all sides of the vehicle before beginning to drive.

Day 18/Page 133: 1. $x = -1, -5$; 2. $x = 2, 6$; 3. $x = 2, 8$; 4. Yes, when $x = 4$ is substituted into the equation, $y = 0$, so this is a solution of the given quadratic equation.; 5. No, when $x = 7$ is substituted into the equation, y does not equal 0, so $x = 7$ is not a solution of the given quadratic equation.; 6. frightening: dark and stormy, alone in the darkness; 7. anxious: deep breath, stomach in knots, squeezing her eyes shut; 8. embarrassed: cheeks burning, eyes stinging; 9. C; 10. D; 11. Student answers will vary.

Day 19/Page 135: 1. 0.68; 2. 0.6; 3. 0.61; 4. 0.5; 5. 0.76; 6. 1.17; 7. 2.2; 8. 0.75; 9. C; 10. delete ", including"; 11. change the colon to a comma; 12. delete the colon; 13. C; 14. C; 15. delete ", for example"; 16. B; 17. D; 18. B; 19. A; 20. S: Jason, DO: (a) bath, IO: (our) dog; 21. S: I, DO: (five) books, IO: none; 22. S: (my) mother, DO: lasagna, IO: me; 23. S: Coach Johnson, DO: (a pep) talk, IO: (his) team; 24. S: Laura, DO: (first) prize, IO: none; 25. S: We, DO: (the family) portrait, IO: none; 26. S: Tom, DO: (the lilac) bush, IO: plenty (of water and plant food); 27. S: T.S. Eliot, DO: (the) Nobel Prize for Literature, IO: none

Day 20/Page 137: 1. $39.50; 2. 35,000 people; 3. $32.40; 4. $9.38; 5–6. Answers may vary. 5. *Pride and Prejudice*, my favorite novel, was written more than 200 years ago.; 6. *Pride and Prejudice*, which is my favorite novel, was written more than 200 years ago.; Jade: golf cart; Brenna: skateboard; Finn: roller skates; Tiana: bicycle; Tony: scooter; 7. elections; 8. poll taxes; 9. suffrage; 10. sex; 11. eighteen; 12. race

Bonus Page 139: 1. Yes, in theory the temperature should increase as the number of hours of daylight increases. This might vary if there is too much cloud cover.; 2. Yes, higher winds make for lower temperatures. This may vary in tropical locations where it is consistently hot and windy, or polar locations where it is consistently cold and windy.

Bonus Page 140: Answers will vary.

Bonus Page 141: 1. South Carolina; 2. New Hampshire; 3. Virginia; 4. Delaware; 5. Connecticut; 6. Georgia; 7. Massachusetts; 8. Pennsylvania; 9. New York; 10. Rhode Island; 11. North Carolina; 12. New Jersey; 13. Maryland

Bonus Page 142: Student answers may vary. 1. bans cruel and unusual punishment and excessive fines/bail; 2. rights not limited to only those listed in the Constitution; 3. federal government only has the rights designated by the Constitution, and other rights are those of the local and state governments

Bonus Page 143: 1. N; 2. K; 3. B; 4. I; 5. D; 6. C; 7. F; 8. O; 9. J; 10. H; 11. M.; 12. A; 13. P; 14. G; 15. Q; 16. E; 17. L

bioluminescence illuminate luminous	amphibian amphibious amphitheater	durable duration endure
benediction benefactor beneficial	verdict verify veritable	determine exterminate terminal
circulate circumstance encircle	telephone telescope television	malady malevolent malicious

biography biology bionic	autoimmune automobile automated	cordial coronary discord
rough : texture :: spicy : __food__	ornate : simple :: amiable : __unfriendly__	buoyant : __floats__ :: luminous : shines
tenant : apartment :: __bear/bat__ : cave	__bibliography__ : books :: roster : names	lion : pride :: elephant : __herd__

attorney : courtroom :: _____ : animal hospital	bleach : clean :: oil : _____	Statue of Liberty : landmark :: Australia : _____
avert : eyes :: shuffle : _____	cosmetic : lipstick :: _____ : scarf	allowed : aloud :: _____ : principal
aroma : _____ :: harmonious : sound	crescent : moon :: _____ : kite	encore : play :: epilogue : _____

Statue of Liberty : landmark :: Australia : __continent__	bleach : clean :: oil : __cook__	attorney : courtroom :: veterinarian : animal hospital
allowed : aloud :: __principle__ : principal	cosmetic : lipstick :: __accessory__ : scarf	avert : eyes :: shuffle : __feet__
encore : play :: epilogue : __book__	crescent : moon :: __diamond/rhombus__ : kite	aroma : __smell__ :: harmonious : sound

Lindsay likes light-colored llamas.	We waited for days in the line.	They were as <u>fast as lightning</u>.
I went to the store.	You went to the store.	They went to the store.
credibility/trust	emotion	logic/reason

© Carson Dellosa

$\sqrt{196} =$ ___	$\sqrt{10{,}000} =$ ___	$5^4 =$ ___
$\sqrt{6{,}400} =$ ___	$\sqrt{1{,}144} =$ ___	$11^{-4} =$ ___
$\sqrt{289} =$ ___	$\sqrt[3]{125} =$ ___	$(-3)^3 =$ ___

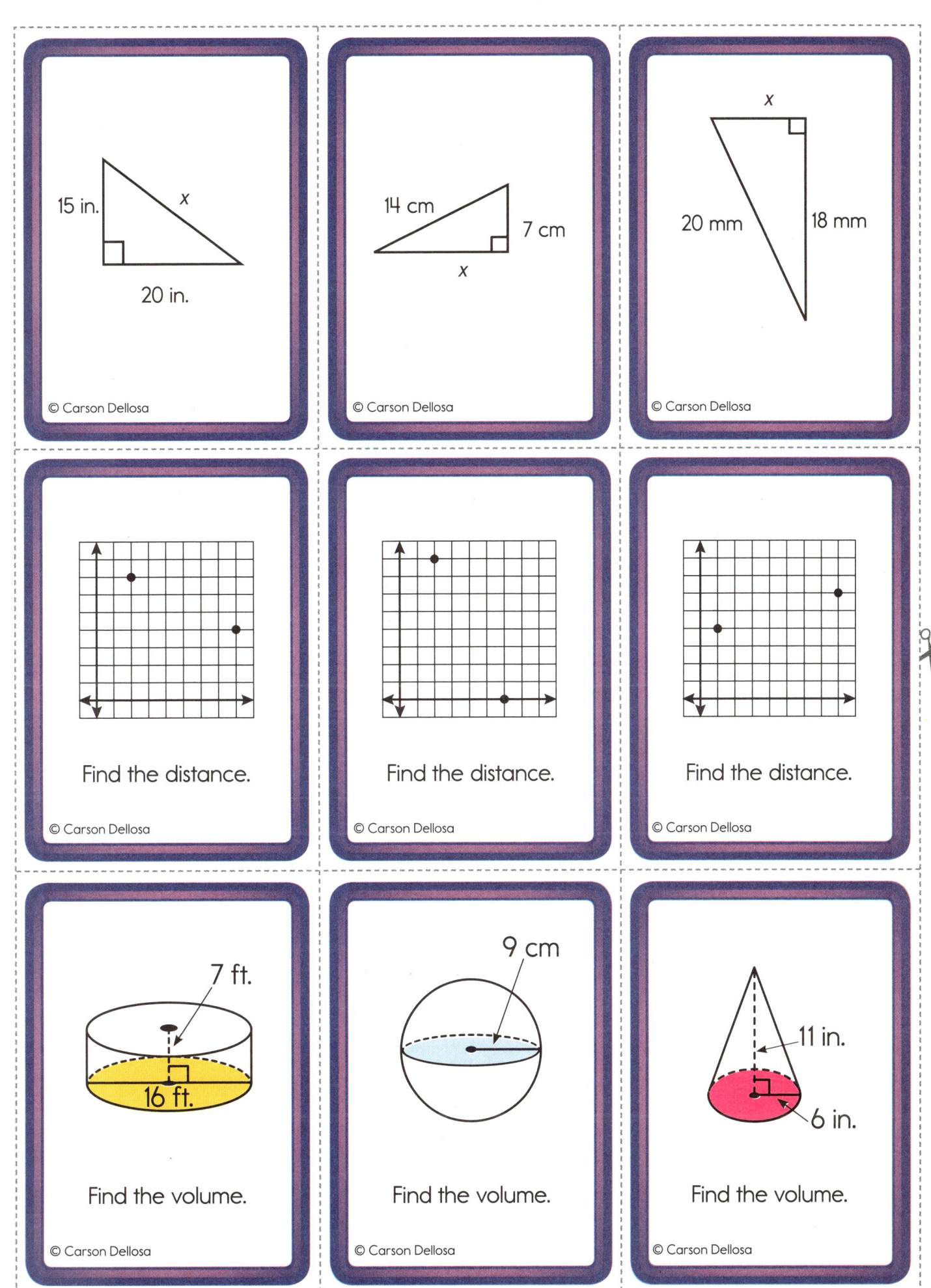

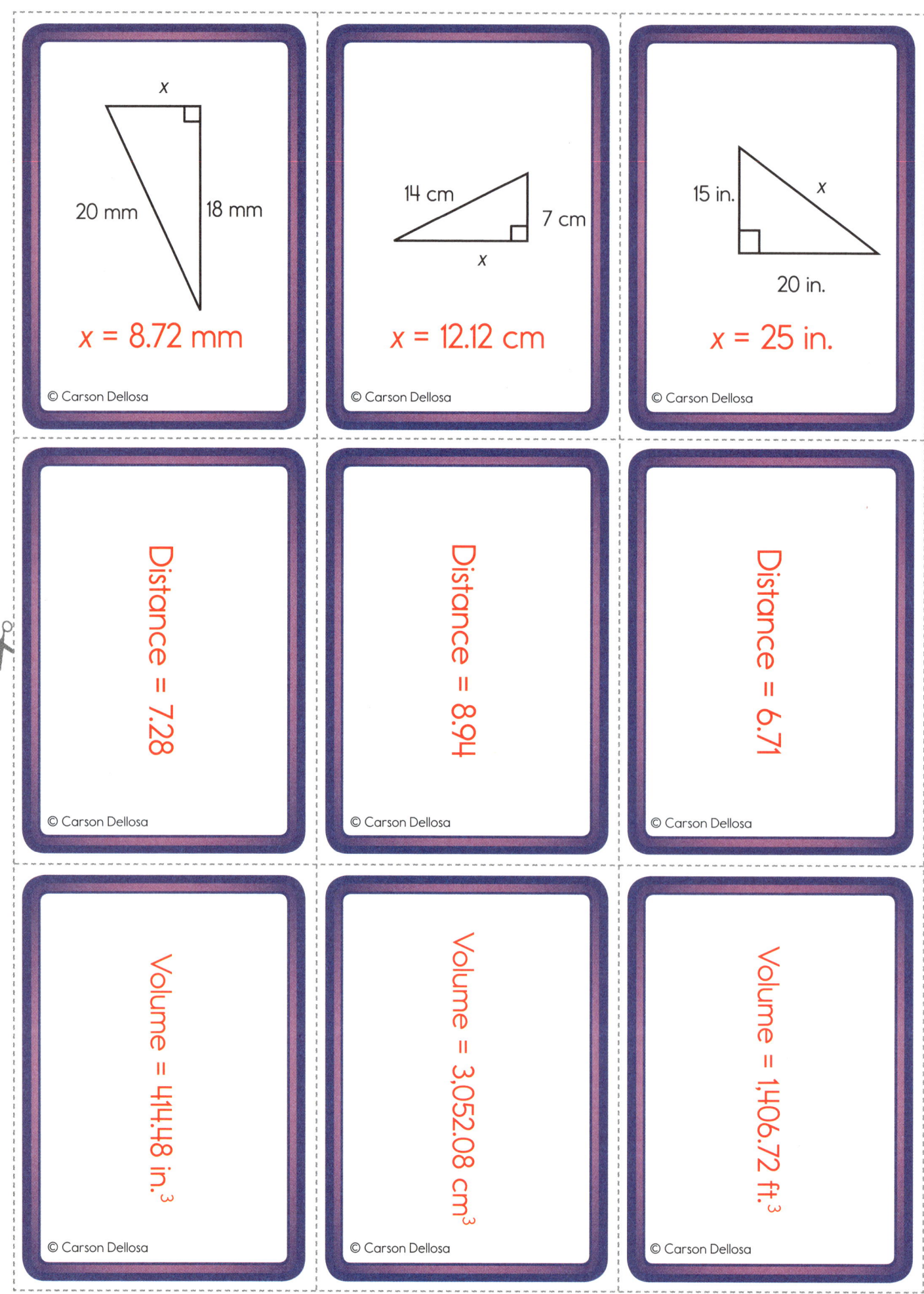

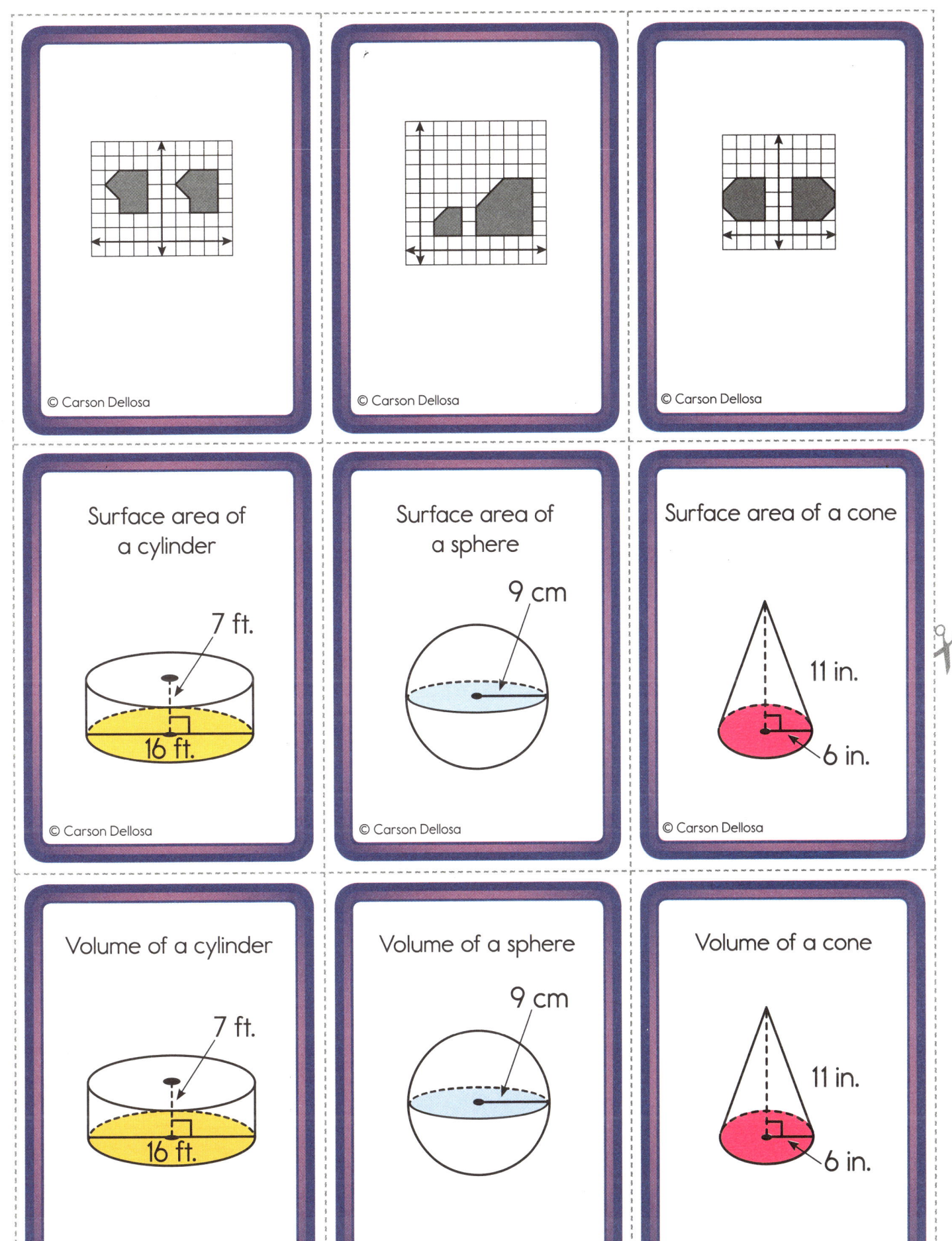

reflection	dilation	translation
$SA = \pi r(r + \sqrt{h^2 + r^2})$	$SA = 4\pi r^2$	$SA = 2\pi rh + 2\pi r^2$
$V = \frac{1}{3}\pi r^2 h$	$V = \frac{4}{3}\pi r^3$	$V = \pi r^2 h$

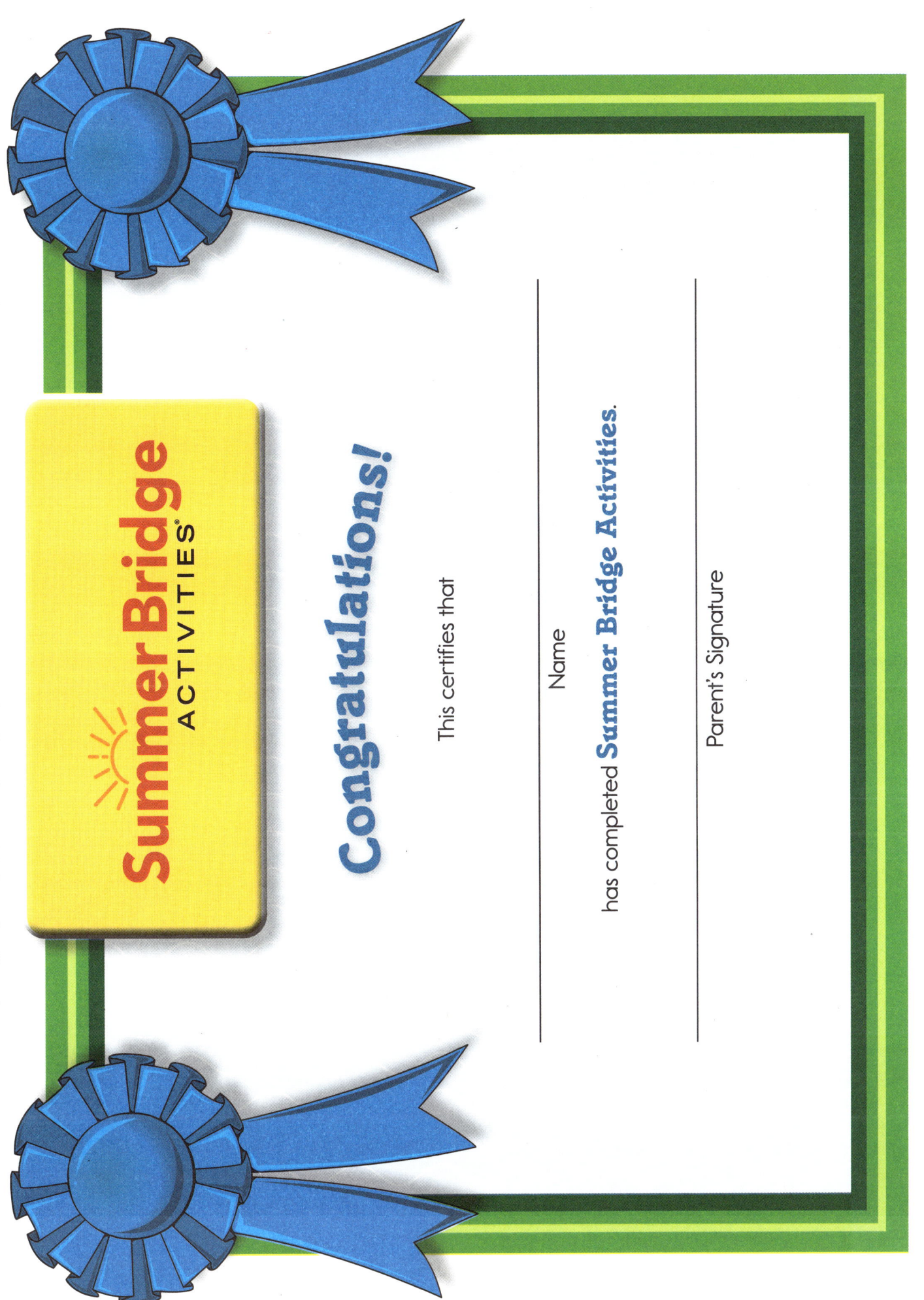